murach's
AI-Assisted Programming with Copilot

Mary Delamater

Scott McCoy

MIKE MURACH & ASSOCIATES, INC.

3730 W Swift Ave. • Fresno, CA 93722

www.murach.com • murachbooks@murach.com

Editorial team

Authors:	Mary Delamater
	Scott McCoy
Editor:	Joel Murach
Production:	Juliette Baylon

Murach also has books on these subjects:

Web development

HTML/CSS

Modern JavaScript

JavaScript and jQuery

PHP and MySQL

ASP.NET Core MVC

Programming languages

Python

Java

C#

C++

Databases

MySQL

SQL Server

Oracle

Data science

Python for Data Science

R for Data Analysis

For more on Murach books, please visit us at www.murach.com

© 2025, Mike Murach & Associates, Inc.

Printed in the United States of America

10 9 8 7 6 5 4 3 2 1
ISBN: 978-1-943873-23-4

Contents

Introduction   ix

Section 1 Get started with Copilot

Chapter 1   Create two short programs   3
Chapter 2   The essential skills for using Copilot   37

Section 2 More skills as you need them

Chapter 3   Create a Python program   67
Chapter 4   Create a website   101
Chapter 5   Work with a database   129
Chapter 6   Design and maintain software   147
Chapter 7   Implement unit testing   173

Expanded contents

Section 1 Get started with Copilot

Chapter 1 Create two short programs

Background terms and concepts 4
Some important terms 4
An introduction to AI assistants 5
Four components of an AI assistant 6

How to set up your computer 7
Download the files for this book 7
Install VS Code 8
Enable Copilot 8
Install Python 9
Set up VS Code 9

How to create a web app 12
Generate the code 12
Test the code thoroughly 20
Improve the code 23

How to create a Python program 25
Generate the code 25
Test the code thoroughly 27
Improve the code 28

A review and a look forward 31
The prompts for the Python program 31
Problems with LLMs 33

Chapter 2 The essential skills for using Copilot

How to edit files 38
Use the Chat window in Ask mode 38
Use the Chat window in Edit mode 40
Use the Chat window in Agent mode 42
Use inline chat 43
Use comment prompts 44
How to choose which technique to use 45

How to use chat participants and slash commands 47
Use chat participants 47
Use slash commands 51

Best practices for prompt engineering 54
Be specific 54
Provide context 55
Specify output 55
Say what to do 55
Assign roles 56
Use structured formats 57

Types of prompts **58**
Zero-shot.. 58
Few-shot... 58
Prompt chaining.. 59
Chain of thought 61
More types of prompts... 62

Section 2 More skills as you need them

Chapter 3 Create a Python program

How to use Python doctests with Copilot **68**
How to add a doctest to a function.. 68
How to run doctests.. 69
How to use Copilot to write doctests 70
How to simulate user input or random numbers 71

Generate the initial code **74**
Make a plan in the Chat window.. 74
Apply the code to the files 77
Run the program 78
Run the doctests... 79

Improve the initial code **82**
Add a graphical representation of a die... 82
Format the player scores... 87
Format the player turn 90

Refactor the code **94**
Ask Copilot for advice... 94
Convert from functions to objects.. 94
Run the program 97

Chapter 4 Create a website

Start the website.. **100**
Examine the starting files.. 100
Create a directory structure... 101
Develop the home page... 103
Develop a speaker page 106

Refine the web pages.. **107**
Fix the content for the home page 107
Refine the shared code... 108
Refine the header 109

Fix two responsive design issues **111**
Scale the images 111
Add a menu toggle for small screens 113

Refactor the website **117**
Use nested styles.. 118
Add a submenu to the navbar 120
Add comments to HTML and CSS files 125

Chapter 5   Work with a database

How to work with SQLite...128
Install DB Browser for SQLite 128
Open a database and view its tables... 128
Run SQL statements 130
Export a schema 131

Work with an existing database..132
Select data from a single table... 132
Select data from multiple tables 134
Insert, update, and delete data... 135
Create other types of queries 138
Create transactions 139

Create a new database 140
Generate a script that creates a database.................................... 140
Run the script and test the database 141

Chapter 6   Design and maintain software

How to design new software 144
Gather requirements 144
Make architectural decisions.. 151
Create a project structure 154
Address other planning issues.. 156

How to maintain existing software 157
Analyze existing code 157
Find and fix bugs 159
Find and fix security issues 160
Add comments.. 162
Create a README.md file.. 163

Chapter 7   Implement unit testing

An introduction to unit testing..170

How to unit test Python code..170
Install pytest 171
Generate some initial tests 172
Generate tests for edge cases and more....................................... 176
Troubleshoot failing tests 177

How to unit test JavaScript..181
Install Node.js..181
Install Jest 182
Generate some initial tests 184
Generate tests for edge cases and more....................................... 188
Troubleshoot failing tests 189

How to mock external dependencies..192
Mock a dependency in Python 193
Mock a dependency in JavaScript... 195

How to use test-driven development (TDD) 198
Generate tests for non-existent code 199
Generate code that passes the tests 201
Refactor the code by generating more tests 202

Introduction

Ever since ChatGPT was released in 2022, AI experts have been saying that AI is going to change the way we live and work. Some predict that these changes will be dramatic and transformational. Within the software industry, many programmers are already using AI to write code. This trend is bound to continue as AI assistants for developing software continue to get better.

GitHub Copilot is one of the leading AI assistants for developing software. When used correctly, Copilot can help you develop software more quickly than ever before. In addition, it can help you develop software that's of a higher quality. In some cases, it can even help you create software that you wouldn't be able to create without AI.

Who this book is for

In general, this book is for anyone who wants to learn how to use an AI assistant to develop software. More specifically, this book is for anyone who wants to learn how to use GitHub Copilot to develop software.

This book shows how to use Copilot to create software using programming languages like HTML, CSS, JavaScript, Python, and SQL. However, most of the concepts and skills presented in this book also apply to other programming languages, libraries, and frameworks. For example, if you need to develop code in a language like C++ or Java, most of the concepts and skills presented in this book still apply. Or, if you need to use a library like React or a framework like Node.js, most of the concepts and skills presented in this book still apply.

Prerequisite

The only prerequisite for this book is a basic understanding of HTML, CSS, and at least one programming language like JavaScript or Python. That's because being able to understand code is still necessary when you're using AI to develop software.

Although AI often generates excellent code that works as expected, it can also generate low-quality code that doesn't work correctly or at all. As a result, the generated code still needs to be reviewed and thoroughly tested by a human. And if there are problems with the code, the human needs to ask the right questions and enter the right prompts to guide the AI to fix the problems. In other words, even with AI, it still takes a human who understands coding to create quality software.

Recommended software

To work with GitHub Copilot, we recommend using Visual Studio Code (VS Code) as your integrated development environment (IDE). That's because VS Code works with most languages and runs on most modern operating systems. More importantly, it's easy to use Copilot from within VS Code. It's possible to use Copilot from within several other IDEs, but we recommend using VS Code as shown in this book.

The downloadable files

You can download all the files you need to get the most from this book from our website (www.murach.com) as described in chapter 1. These files include the code for the programs, websites, and databases that we present throughout this book. This makes it easy for you to review this code. In addition, you can use these files as starting points for some of the exercises at the end of each chapter. Then, you can use Copilot to further improve them.

Please send us your thoughts

For many people, the recent advances AI are exciting because they raise so many new possibilities. For others, these advances induce anxiety because they're likely to change the way we live and work. With this book, we have done our best to demystify AI-assisted programming by helping you learn how to use Copilot.

If you have time, please send us your thoughts on this book. We're always interested in what you have to say about our books, and we always do our best to use your feedback to improve future editions.

Thanks!

Joel Murach

Joel Murach
Editor

Section 1

Get started with Copilot

AI assistants like GitHub Copilot are changing the way developers write code. As a result, if you want to develop software, it's important to understand how to use an AI assistant like Copilot.

This section gets you off to a fast start with Copilot. To do that, the first chapter dives right in and shows how to use Copilot to create two short programs, a web app that uses JavaScript and a command-line Python program. Then, the second chapter presents some of the essential skills for using Copilot. In addition, it describes some best practices for writing prompts for AI. These practices apply to all AI assistants, not just Copilot.

Chapter 1

Create two short programs

This chapter shows how to use Copilot to create two short programs, a simple web app that uses JavaScript to perform a calculation, and a command-line Python program that performs the same calculation. But first, this chapter introduces some important background terms and concepts, and it shows how to set up your computer to work with Copilot.

Due to the nature of LLMs, you won't be able to follow along with this chapter on your system. In other words, even if you copy the prompts exactly, you will almost certainly get different responses with different code. As a result, you might not encounter the issues described in this chapter, and you may encounter other issues. However, the concepts and skills presented in this chapter should help you handle these issues. So, if you keep entering prompts, you should be able to develop the programs described in this chapter.

Background terms and concepts	**4**
Some important terms	4
An introduction to AI assistants	5
Four components of an AI assistant	6
How to set up your computer	**7**
Download the files for this book	7
Install VS Code	8
Enable Copilot	8
Install Python	9
Set up VS Code	9
How to create a web app	**12**
Generate the code	12
Test the code thoroughly	20
Improve the code	23
How to create a Python program	**25**
Generate the code	25
Test the code thoroughly	27
Improve the code	28
A review and a look forward	**31**
The prompts for the Python program	31
Problems with LLMs	33
Perspective	**34**

Background terms and concepts

Before you start using Copilot to generate code, you should be aware of some important background terms and concepts that apply to AI.

Some important terms

Generally speaking, *artificial intelligence (AI)* is when machines like computers act intelligently. Within AI, there are several fields of study.

Machine learning. Within AI, researchers use *machine learning (ML)* to develop statistical algorithms that can learn from data and then make predictions about data that they have never seen. This allows a computer to perform tasks that they haven't been programmed to handle. For example, an algorithm that's designed to identify whether an image contains a cat is trained on a large number of images but performs this task on images that it has never seen before.

Deep learning. Within machine learning, *deep learning* uses neural networks, a class of statistical algorithms, to surpass many previous machine learning approaches in performance.

Generative AI. Within deep learning, *generative AI* generates text, code, images, audio, video, or other forms of data.

Large language model (LLM). Within generative AI, a *large language model (LLM)* is designed for *natural language processing (NLP)* tasks such as language generation. An LLM is trained on vast amounts of data to understand patterns and relationships between words. This allows it to generate human-like text, answer questions, translate languages, summarize information, and even write different creative content based on prompts.

Although an LLM is trained on vast amounts of data, it's just a statistical model that predicts what should come next. To do that, it breaks text down into small units called *tokens*, which are roughly equivalent to a word or a part of a word.

For example, given a sentence that starts with "Paris is a city in", an LLM will most likely predict that "France" is the next word. However, given a sentence that starts with "London is," the LLM will most likely give you significantly different answers every time. That's because there are many more possible answers for the second prompt, and most LLMs add a little randomness to their answers.

A *generative pretrained transformer (GPT)* is a type of LLM. Modern GPTs can be fine-tuned for specific tasks. For example, ChatGPT is fine-tuned to process language in a way that allows it to chat with a user.

An introduction to AI assistants

An *AI assistant*, or *AI agent*, provides an interface that allows you to interact with an LLM. By now, you've probably heard about some of the AI assistants in the following list. That's probably because the launch of ChatGPT in 2022 caused a boom in interest in AI. This boom led to the development of more AI assistants that provide access to powerful LLMs.

Three AI assistants

- ChatGPT
- Copilot
- Claude

These are just three of the many AI assistants available today. All three can generate code in just about any programming language, but this book focuses on Copilot. However, many of the skills for working with Copilot also apply to other LLMs such as ChatGPT and Claude.

When you enter a *prompt* into an AI assistant and send the prompt to the LLM, it generates a *response* and returns it to you. For example, you can enter a prompt into ChatGPT using a web interface as shown next.

ChatGPT with a prompt

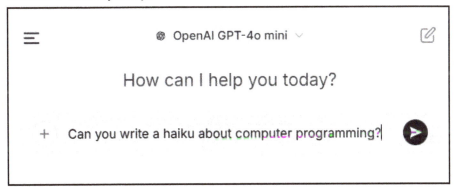

This web interface shows that ChatGPT is using an LLM called GPT-4o mini. This LLM uses a GPT developed by OpenAI, an American AI research organization. When you use ChatGPT to send the prompt to the LLM, the LLM returns a response like the one shown next.

ChatGPT with a prompt and a response

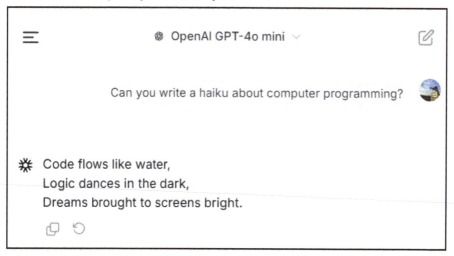

In the response, the poem follows the rules of a haiku (5 syllables in the first line, 7 in the second, and 5 in the third) and is about computer programming as requested by the prompt. The response might not be great poetry, but it was generated by AI in a matter of seconds, much faster than most humans could write a haiku of similar quality.

At this point, you can enter more prompts. When you do, the LLM takes all of the previous prompts and responses in the chat into consideration. This is known as the chat's *context*, or *working memory*. As a result, you can chat with an LLM in the way that you chat with a person, and the LLM's responses often improve as the prompts and responses give it more context.

If you're following along as you read, you should realize that the response generated by ChatGPT most likely won't be the same for you, even if you use the same LLM. That's because if you send the same prompt to an LLM multiple times, the LLM does not generate the same response every time. It may generate a similar response, but it's unlikely to be exactly the same. In other words, with an LLM, the input does not determine the output. This is known as being *nondeterministic*.

By contrast, if you send the same Python code to a compiler multiple times, the compiler generates the same output every time. In other words, the input determines the output. This is known as being *deterministic*.

Four components of an AI assistant

An AI assistant has the following four components.

Model. An AI assistant typically uses a large language model (LLM) to generate its responses. When you use an AI assistant like Copilot, you can select the type of model that you're using. By default, it uses the GPT-4o model that's also used by ChatGPT, but you can select other models too.

Tools. An AI assistant's tools can consist of function calling interfaces, APIs, system commands, or other tools that the AI assistant is allowed to use. Different AI assistants have access to different sets of tools which make some assistants better at certain tasks than others. For example, Copilot includes tools that make it optimal for working with code such as a feature that allows you to accept or reject suggested changes to your code files.

Context window. As described earlier, an AI assistant's context window keeps track of the current chat. This includes all of the previous prompts and responses, and it may also include external files such as code files.

Planning/reasoning systems. An AI assistant's *planning and reasoning systems* are responsible for breaking down tasks into manageable steps, deciding which tools to use, handling unexpected results or errors, and chaining actions together to solve a problem.

Reasoning systems are especially important for questions involving math, science and computer programming. Recently, there have been many advances in reasoning systems. As a result, AI has been improving at math, science, and computer programming.

How to set up your computer

Now that you know some important terms and concepts, you're ready to set up your computer to use it with this book. That includes setting up GitHub Copilot so you can use it with Visual Studio Code (VS Code). In addition, since many of the examples in this book use the Python language, you should also install Python if it isn't already installed on your computer.

Download the files for this book

The download for this book includes files for the examples and programs the book presents. As a result, if you want to view these examples or run these programs, you should download these files as shown here:

How to download the files for this book

1. Go to www.murach.com and find the page for this book.
2. Scroll down to the "FREE downloads" tab and click it.
3. Click the Download Now button for the zip file. This should download a zip file.
4. Double-click the zip file. This should create a folder named copilot.
5. Move the copilot folder to the correct folder. We recommend putting it in a folder named murach within your Documents folder, but you can put it wherever you like.

Install VS Code

This book shows how to use Copilot from within an integrated development environment (IDE). In particular, it shows how to use Copilot from within Visual Studio Code, also known as VS Code. As a result, if you want to follow along with this book, you can install VS Code as described here:

How to install VS Code

1. Download the installer file from https://code.visualstudio.com/download.
2. Double-click the installer file. This should run the installer program.
3. Respond to the resulting dialogs. You can accept the default options.

VS Code can be used to write code in most languages including HTML, CSS, JavaScript, Python, and more. As a result, it's a great IDE for many types of development.

If you want to use another IDE, Copilot can also be used from within many other IDEs including Visual Studio, Eclipse, and Xcode. However, this book only shows how to use Copilot from within VS Code.

Enable Copilot

Copilot is available from the GitHub website (www.github.com) that Microsoft currently owns. This website provides a platform that allows developers to store, manage, and share their code. It hosts many open-source software projects and is considered by many to be the world's largest host of source code.

At this time of this writing, Copilot is automatically enabled for all GitHub accounts by default. As a result, if you have a GitHub account, you should be able to begin using the free version of Copilot right away. However, if Copilot isn't enabled on your system, you can enable it by using the following steps.

How to enable Copilot

1. Sign in to your GitHub account. If you don't already have an account, go to www.github.com and create one.
2. Click the profile icon that's at the top right corner. This should display a drop-down menu.
3. Select "Your Copilot". This should display the settings for Copilot.
4. Make sure the "Show Copilot" option is enabled. If necessary, enter any payment information. At the time of this writing, Copilot is available for free.
5. If you want access to the Pro plan, click "Start a free trial". Then, select the plan and enter your payment information.

At the time of this writing, Copilot is free for 50 chat messages per month. The free version provides other restrictions as well, but it works well enough to get started.

If you pass the usage limits, you can sign up for a free one-month trial of Copilot Pro. This provides extensive usage and other benefits. At the time of this writing, Copilot Pro is $20 per month after the free trial ends.

Install Python

Many of the examples in this book use the Python language. As a result, if you want to follow along, you can install Python on your computer as described below.

How to install Python

1. Download the installer file from https://www.python.org/downloads/. Make sure to download the latest version of Python that's available for your system.
2. Double-click the installer file. This should run the installer program.
3. If you're using Windows, check the "Add Python to PATH" box.
4. Respond to the resulting dialogs. You can accept the default options. This should install Python.
5. Test your system. To do that, double-click on the future_value.py file in the copilot/ch01/python folder. If this runs the Future Value program, Python is installed correctly.

Set up VS Code

To set up VS Code so it can work with Copilot and Python, we recommend the Copilot and Python extensions shown next. In addition, we recommend the Open in Browser extension from TechER that makes it easy to use VS Code to open an HTML file in a browser.

Extensions for working with Copilot

- GitHub Copilot
- GitHub Copilot Chat

Extensions for working with Python

- Python
- Pylance
- Python Debugger

An extension for running an HTML file

- Open in Browser (from TechER)

To install these extensions, you can use this procedure:

How to install an extension

1. Start VS Code.
2. Click the Extensions icon in the left sidebar.
3. Find the extension. To do that, type the name of the extension in the text box at the top of the Extensions window. This should filter the available extensions.
4. Select the extension and click the Install button. This should install the extension.

As you follow this procedure, installing one extension often installs another. For example, when you install the GitHub Copilot extension, it may install the GitHub Copilot Chat extension. Similarly, when you install the Python extension, it may install the Pylance and Python Debugger extensions. When you're done installing these extensions, the VS Code's Extensions window should look something like the following screen.

VS Code with the Copilot extensions installed

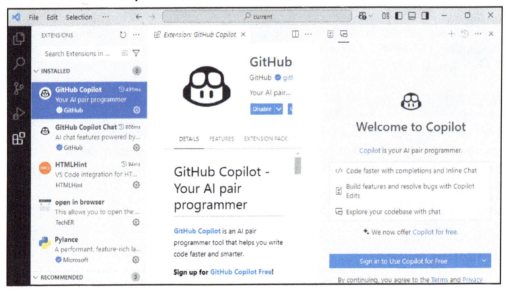

Before you start using Copilot to generate code, you may want to provide Copilot with some standing instructions about coding conventions that you want to use. For example, I like to limit each line of code to 80 characters or less because that's generally considered a good practice since it makes code easier to read and review.

To add code generation instructions to Copilot, you can open the settings.json file as shown next.

How to set up instructions for code generation

1. Start VS Code.
2. Select File ▶ Preferences ▶ Settings to display the Settings dialog.
3. Select Extensions ▶ GitHub Copilot Chat ▶ Experimental.
4. Find the Code Generation Instructions section and click the "Edit in settings.json" link.

After you open the settings.json file, you can use VS Code to add an instruction to the JSON file as shown next.

An instruction for limiting each line of generated code to 80 characters or less

```
"github.copilot.chat.codeGeneration.instructions": [
{
    "text": "Limit code lines to a maximum of 80 characters."
}
]
```

When you modify the settings.json file, you can add any instructions you want. However, since these instructions are passed to Copilot with each prompt, you should keep them short and precise or they may degrade Copilot's performance.

How to create a web app

Now that you have your system set up, you're ready to use Copilot with VS Code to create a program. To get you started, this chapter shows how to use Copilot to develop a simple web app that calculates the future value of a series of monthly payments for a specified number of years at a given interest rate.

Generate the code

There are several ways you can generate the code for a web app. For this chapter, I decided to use VS Code to open a Chat window as shown next.

How to open a Chat window

1. Start VS Code.
2. Open the folder you want to use. To do that, you can select File ▶ Open Folder from the menu system.
3. Open a Chat window. To do that, you can select Open Chat from the Copilot icon in the title bar. Or, you can press Ctrl+Alt+I (Windows) or Cmd+Alt+I (macOS).

When you open a Chat window for the first time, it should be empty as shown next.

A Chat window that's ready for a prompt

By default, the Chat window begins with a message that explains that mistakes are possible. As explained earlier, that's unavoidable due to the way that LLMs work, and it's why you need to carefully test code that's generated by Copilot.

In addition, it indicates that you can click on the paperclip icon to attach files such as code files that give the Chat window the context it needs to help you write code. It indicates that you can click on the @ icon to chat with Copilot extensions, and you can type a front slash (/) to enter a command. For now, I'm not going to use these techniques, but the next chapter explains how to use them.

At this point, you can use the Chat window to ask Copilot questions or give it specifications by entering text into the prompt at the bottom of the window. For example, I entered the following question and specifications to start the Future Value web app.

A prompt for starting the Future Value web app

Can you create a web page that calculates the future value of a series of monthly payments over a specified number of years at a given interest rate?

Here are some specifications:
* Get the monthly payment, years, and interest rate from the user.
* Use this input to calculate the future value.
* Store the HTML, CSS, and JavaScript for the page in separate files.

To enter this prompt, I used Shift+Enter to enter line breaks. That's because pressing Enter sends the prompt to Copilot for processing. After I typed this prompt and pressed Enter, Copilot gave me the response shown next.

The response from Copilot

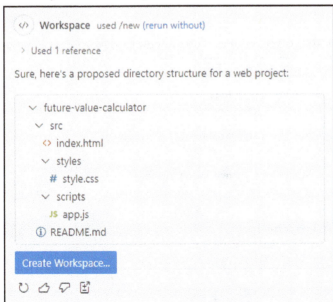

I reviewed the suggested directory structure, and I thought it looked good enough, so I clicked on the Create Workspace button. This created the following directory structure in the Explorer window.

The directory structure in the Explorer window

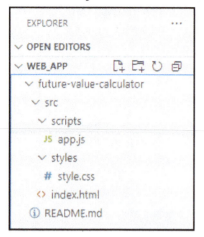

In addition, it generated the following code for the HTML, CSS, and JavaScript files needed by this web app.

The HTML generated by Copilot

```html
<!DOCTYPE html>
<html lang="en">
<head>
    <meta charset="UTF-8">
    <meta name="viewport" content="width=device-width, initial-scale=1.0">
    <title>Future Value Calculator</title>
    <link rel="stylesheet" href="styles/style.css">
</head>
<body>
    <div class="container">
        <h1>Future Value Calculator</h1>
        <label for="monthlyPayment">Monthly Payment:</label>
        <input type="number" id="monthlyPayment" required>

        <label for="years">Number of Years:</label>
        <input type="number" id="years" required>

        <label for="interestRate">Annual Interest Rate (%):</label>
        <input type="number" id="interestRate" required>

        <button id="calculateBtn">Calculate Future Value</button>

        <h2 id="result"></h2>
    </div>
    <script src="scripts/app.js"></script>
</body>
</html>
```

The CSS generated by Copilot

```css
body {
    font-family: Arial, sans-serif;
    margin: 0;
    padding: 20px;
    background-color: #f4f4f4;
}

h1 {
    color: #333;
}

.container {
    max-width: 600px;
    margin: auto;
    background: #fff;
    padding: 20px;
    border-radius: 5px;
    box-shadow: 0 2px 10px rgba(0, 0, 0, 0.1);
}

input[type="number"],
input[type="button"] {
    width: 100%;
    padding: 10px;
    margin: 10px 0;
    border: 1px solid #ccc;
    border-radius: 5px;
}

input[type="button"] {
    background-color: #28a745;
    color: white;
    cursor: pointer;
}

input[type="button"]:hover {
    background-color: #218838;
}

.result {
    margin-top: 20px;
    font-size: 1.2em;
    color: #333;
}
```

The JavaScript generated by Copilot

```javascript
// JavaScript logic for future value calculator

function calculateFutureValue() {
    const monthlyPayment = parseFloat(document.getElementById('payment').value);
    const years = parseFloat(document.getElementById('years').value);
    const interestRate = parseFloat(document.getElementById('rate').value) / 100;

    if (isNaN(monthlyPayment) || isNaN(years) || isNaN(interestRate)) {
        alert('Please enter valid numbers.');
        return;
    }

    const months = years * 12;
    const futureValue = monthlyPayment *
        (((1 + interestRate / 12) ** months - 1) / (interestRate / 12));

    document.getElementById('result').innerText =
        `Future Value: $${futureValue.toFixed(2)}`;
}

document.getElementById('calculate')
        .addEventListener('click', calculateFutureValue);
```

I read through this code to determine if it creates the Future Value web app that I specified, and I decided that it might. However, I'd rather use a loop to calculate the future value than the formula. To do that, I entered the following prompt.

A prompt for modifying the code

> That's pretty good, but I'd like to use a loop to calculate the future value. Can you do that?

This shows that you can't expect Copilot or any other AI assistant to generate code that's exactly what you want on its first attempt. Instead, Copilot learns from its first attempt and improves on later attempts. That's because Copilot remembers all of the prompts and responses in the chat. Taken together, this is known as the context for the chat. As a result, Copilot's responses improve as you provide more context with your prompts.

When I sent the previous prompt to Copilot, it displayed the following response.

A response with the modified code

Sure, here's the updated ⟨JS⟩ app.js file using a loop to calculate the future value:

```javascript
// JavaScript logic for future value calculator

function calculateFutureValue() {
    const monthlyPayment = parseFloat(document.getElementById
    const years = parseFloat(document.getElementById('years')
    const interestRate = parseFloat(document.getElementById('i

    if (isNaN(monthlyPayment) || isNaN(years) || isNaN(intere
```

Although you can't see it in this response, this JavaScript uses a loop to calculate the future value. As a result, I decided to apply it to the JavaScript file. To do that, I scrolled up to the top of the suggested code and clicked on the Apply icon as shown next.

The icon for applying the code to a file in the code editor

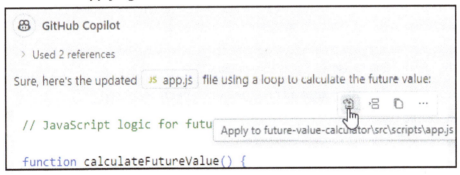

This copied the generated code into the JavaScript file in the code editor window, compared it to the original code, and prompted me to accept or discard the changes as shown next.

The code editor with changes that you can accept or discard

```
13    const months = years * 12;
      const futureValue = monthlyPayment *                    ✓ ↩ ▣
      (((1 + interestRate / 12) ** months - 1) / (interestRate / 1
14    let futureValue = 0;
15
16    for (let i = 0; i < months; i++) {
17        futureValue = (futureValue + monthlyPayment) * (1 + interest
18    }
19
20    document.getElementById('result').innerText =
21        `Future Value: $${futureValue.toFixed(2)}`;
```

In this screen, the new code is highlighted in green, and the code Copilot wants to delete is highlighted in red. At this point, you can accept or discard a single change by hovering the mouse over it and clicking on the Keep (check mark) or Undo (arrow) icon that appears. Or, you can accept or discard all changes by clicking on the Keep or Undo button that's displayed on the floating menu at the bottom of the code editor window.

A floating menu with buttons to Keep or Undo all changes

In this case, there was only one suggested change, and I decided to accept it. In other cases, there might be multiple suggested changes.

After I accepted the suggested change, Copilot changed the JavaScript for the future value calculation to use a loop as shown next.

The future value calculation after all changes have been accepted

```
const months = years * 12;
let futureValue = 0;

for (let i = 0; i < months; i++) {
    futureValue = (futureValue + monthlyPayment) * (1 + interestRate / 12);
}
```

At this point, I had the HTML, CSS, and JavaScript for this web app open in VS Code as shown next.

VS Code with the generated code

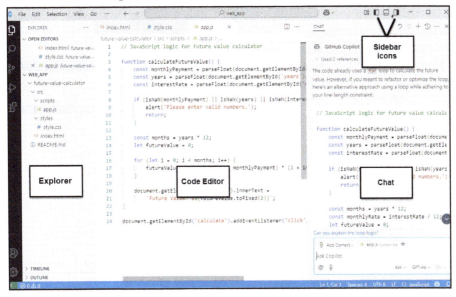

Here, the middle window displays the code editor, the left sidebar displays the Explorer window, and the right sidebar displays the Chat window. The Explorer window shows that the HTML, CSS, and JavaScript for the web app are open, and the Chat window shows the ongoing chat.

If you want to show or hide a sidebar, you can use the icons on the top right corner of the main window. For example, you can click on the icon on the far right to hide the Chat window. Or, you can click on the icon on the far left to hide the Explorer window. I often like to hide the Explorer window to make more space for the code editor and the Chat window.

From this point on, I wanted to allow Copilot to apply its changes directly to the files in the code editor, so I clicked the drop-down arrow to the left of Ask and selected Edit as shown next.

The drop-down list for switching between Ask mode and Edit mode

This switched the Chat window from Ask mode into Edit mode. Since the app.js file is the current file in the code editor, the Chat window displayed this file at the top of the prompt. As a result, the app.js file is part of the context for the prompt. However, if you want to add more files to the context, you can click on the Add Context button to do that. Or, you can right-click on the file in the Explorer window and select Copilot ▶ Add File to Chat.

Test the code thoroughly

Copilot doesn't always generate code that works the way you want. Sometimes, it doesn't even generate code that runs at all. As a result, you need to make sure to test any generated code thoroughly. For a simple web app like this one, you can manually test the code by opening the HTML file in a browser.

If you installed the Open in Browser extension as described earlier in this chapter, you can open an HTML file by right-clicking it in the Explorer window and selecting Open in Default Browser. Or, if the HTML file is the current file in the text editor, you can press the shortcut key of Alt+B.

When I opened the HTML file in a browser, the browser displayed the following web app.

The web app in a browser with a failed calculation

As I reviewed this page, I noticed several formatting issues that I wanted to fix. First, I wanted to improve the appearance of the button. Second, I wanted to add some whitespace between the right side of the text boxes and the right side of the container.

However, this web page looked like it might be able to perform the calculation, so I decided to put the formatting issues on hold and test the app. To start, I entered three values and clicked on the Calculate button. Unfortunately, this didn't display the result of the calculation.

To fix this, I entered the following prompt. But first, I added the HTML file to the context by clicking on Add Context and selecting the files I wanted to add. I did this because I thought that the problem was probably communication between the HTML and JavaScript files. As a result, Copilot probably needed both files as context for this prompt.

A prompt for fixing a bug with two files in the context

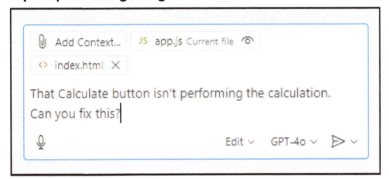

After I entered the prompt, Copilot responded with the following suggestion.

The response with the bug fix

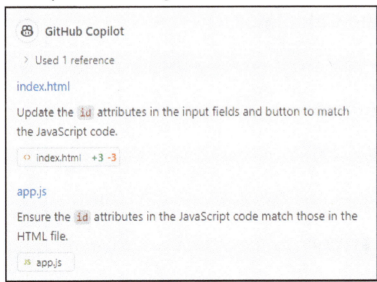

In addition, it suggested the following changes to the HTML file.

The code editor with suggested changes

```
11        <h1>Future Value Calculator</h1>
12        <label for="monthlyPayment">Monthly Payment:</label>
          <input type="number" id="monthlyPayment" required>
13        <input type="number" id="payment" required>
14
15        <label for="years">Number of Years:</label>
16        <input type="number" id="years" required>
17
18        <label for="interestRate">Annual Interest Rate (%):</label>
          <input type="number" id="interestRate" required>
19        <input type="number" id="rate" required>
20
          <button id="calculateBtn">Calculate Future Value</button>
21        <button id="calculate">Calculate Future Value</button>
22
```

This problem often occurs when Copilot is working with multiple files. It's hard to notice when reviewing code because the code in each individual file looks good, but the code isn't coordinated between the files.

At any rate, the suggested changes looked good to me. So, I accepted them, saved the HTML file, refreshed the web page, and entered the calculation again. When I did, the web page calculated the future value as shown next.

The web app with a successful calculation

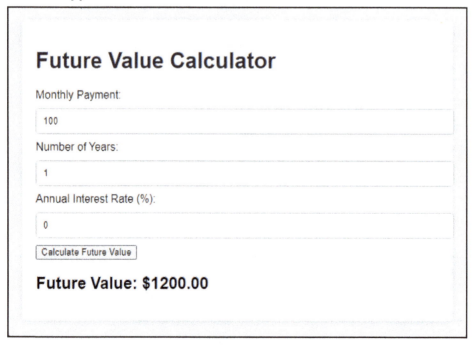

Future Value Calculator

Monthly Payment:

100

Number of Years:

1

Annual Interest Rate (%):

0

Calculate Future Value

Future Value: $1200.00

This calculated a future value of 1200. That's correct since making a monthly payment of 100 for 12 months with an interest rate of 0 is 1200. In this case, I entered an interest rate of zero because it made it easy to test whether the calculation was working correctly.

To test whether the calculation works correctly with a non-zero interest rate, I entered a second calculation. For this calculation, I entered 100 for the payment, 3 for the years, and 3 for the interest rate. This calculated a future value of 3771.46. To verify that this value is correct, I used a spreadsheet to manually perform the calculation.

At this point, the first version of this web app is calculating the future value correctly. That's pretty amazing, considering that I didn't write a single line of code.

To thoroughly test this code, I would also test invalid data as well as very large and small values. Since it's tedious to do this testing manually, I'm not going to do that now. Later, this book presents a technique known as unit testing that lets you automate this kind of testing. In addition, it shows how to use Copilot to help you set up these unit tests.

Improve the code

Although the web app seems to be making the correct calculations, I still wanted improve the formatting for the web app as described next.

Two formatting improvements

- Improve the appearance of the button.
- Add some whitespace between the text boxes and the right side of the container.

When I reviewed the CSS for the web app, it provided styling for the button, but that styling wasn't being applied to the button. So, I entered the following prompt. But first, I made sure the HTML and CSS files were added to the context, since those two files need to work together to provide the formatting.

A prompt for improving the formatting for the button

> The CSS for formatting the Calculate button isn't being applied. Can you fix this?

When I sent this prompt to Copilot, it generated some new code for the CSS file. Then, in the code editor, it displayed the new code in green and the old code in red. I accepted all changes, saved the file, and refreshed the web page to test whether the changes had improved the appearance of the button. When I did, the browser displayed the button like this:

The button with its new formatting

Calculate Future Value

This looked good to me, except that I wanted the font size to be a little larger. So, I entered the following prompt.

A follow-up prompt

> That looks better, but could you make the font size for the button larger?

After I entered this prompt, Copilot suggested adding a line to the CSS file, and I accepted the suggestion. This increased the size of the font to 1.2em, and I thought that improved the appearance of the button.

At this point, I turned my attention to the space between the text boxes and the right side of the container. So, I entered this prompt:

A prompt to add whitespace to the right side of the container

> Can you add some whitespace between the right side of the text boxes and the right side of the container?

After I entered this prompt, Copilot suggested a couple changes to the CSS file, and they looked good to me, so I accepted them. This fixed the display for the text boxes. When I saved the CSS file and refreshed the page, the web app displayed as shown next.

The web app after the improvements are made

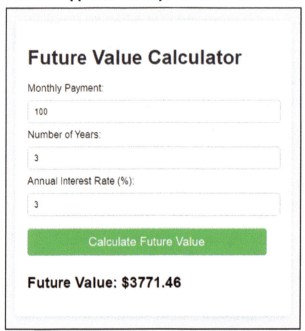

This time, it looked the way I wanted. Hooray!

From here, I decided to pause development of this web app. However, for a production web app, I would consider using unit tests to automate the testing instead of manually testing the web app by running it. Also, I would consider using Copilot to improve this code. For example, I might use Copilot to optimize the HTML for search engines. Or, I might use Copilot to refactor the CSS to use nested styles to make it easier to read and maintain.

How to create a Python program

Now that you've seen how to use Copilot to create a simple web app, this chapter shows how to use many of the same skills to develop a short Python program that performs the same task.

Generate the code

For the Python program, I created a folder to store the program and used VS Code to open that folder. Then, I used VS Code to open a Chat window. This caused Copilot to start a new chat for the new folder in Ask mode. At the bottom of the Chat window, I entered the following prompt.

A prompt for starting the Future Value program

> Can you create a Python program that calculates the future value of a series of monthly payments over a specified number of years at a given interest rate?
>
> Here are some specifications:
> * Use the command line to get input and display output
> * Get the monthly payment, years, and interest rate from the user.
> * Use this input to calculate the future value.
> * Allow the user to continue making calculations until the user chooses to end the program.

This prompt is similar to the prompt for the web app, but it contains a specification to continue making calculations until the user chooses to end the program. When I sent this prompt to Copilot, it gave me a long response that started with the following code

The response from Copilot

Sure, here's a Python program that meets your specifications:

```python
import math

def calculate_future_value(monthly_payment, years, annual_inter
    months = years * 12
    monthly_interest_rate = annual_interest_rate / 12 / 100
    future_value = monthly_payment * ((math.pow(1 + monthly_int
    return future_value

def main():
    while True:
        try:
            monthly_payment = float(input("Enter the monthly pa
            years = int(input("Enter the number of years: "))
            annual_interest_rate = float(input("Enter the annua

            future_value = calculate_future_value(monthly_payme
            print(f"The future value of the series of monthly p

            continue_calculation = input("Do you want to perfor
            if continue_calculation != 'yes':
                break
        except ValueError:
            print("Invalid input. Please enter numeric values f

if __name__ == "__main__":
    main()
```

I read through this code to determine if it creates the Future Value program that I specified, and decided that it might. However, I wanted to use a loop to calculate the future value, not the formula suggested by Copilot. To do that, I entered the following prompt.

A prompt for modifying the code

That's pretty good, but I'd like to use a loop to calculate the future value. Can you do that?

When I sent this prompt to Copilot, it displayed the following response.

A response with the modified code

8 GitHub Copilot

Sure, here's an updated version of the program that uses a loop to calculate the future value:

```python
def calculate_future_value(monthly_payment, years, annual_inter
    months = years * 12
    monthly_interest_rate = annual_interest_rate / 12 / 100
    future_value = 0

    for _ in range(months):
        future_value = (future_value + monthly_payment) * (1 +

    return future_value
```

Since this code does what I want, I decided to create the file to store this program. To do that, I scrolled up to the top of the suggested code, hovered the mouse over it, and clicked the Apply icon. This created a new file in VS Code's editor window and copied the generated code into this file. Then, I saved the file with a name of future_value.py.

Test the code thoroughly

To manually test the code for the Python program, I ran the Python file. To run a Python file, you can click the Run Python File button that's at the top of the code editor. Or, if you want to set up a keyboard shortcut for running a Python file, you can use the following procedure to do that. I like to use Alt+R, but you can use whatever keystroke you prefer.

How to set a keyboard shortcut for running a Python file

1. From the menu system, select File ▶ Preferences ▶ Keyboard Shortcuts.
2. Enter "run python" and double-click on Run Python File.
3. Press the keystroke shortcut you want to use.

When you run a Python file, VS Code displays a Terminal window across the bottom of the screen and runs the program within that window. I tested the program by entering the same two calculations that I used for the web app version of this program. When I was done, the Terminal window looked like the following window.

The Terminal window after two calculations have been made

```
PROBLEMS    OUTPUT    TERMINAL    ...        >_ Python + ∨  ⬚ 🗑 ...  ∧  ✕

& C:/Users/joelm/AppData/Local/Programs/Python/Python310/python.exe c:/Users/
joelm/Documents/murach/copilot/ch01/python/future_value.py
Enter the monthly payment: 100
Enter the number of years: 1
Enter the annual interest rate (as a percentage): 0
The future value of the series of monthly payments is: $1200.00
Do you want to perform another calculation? (yes/no): yes
Enter the monthly payment: 100
Enter the number of years: 3
Enter the annual interest rate (as a percentage): 3
The future value of the series of monthly payments is: $3771.46
Do you want to perform another calculation? (yes/no): no
PS C:\Users\joelm\Documents\murach\copilot\ch01\python> ▌
```

After the first calculation, I entered "yes" to continue to a second calculation. After the second calculation, I entered "no" to end the program. At this point, the first version of this program is calculating the future value correctly.

Improve the code

Although the program is making the correct calculations, I found the user interface to be unfriendly and hard to read. To fix that, I wanted to make the following changes.

Four formatting improvements

- Improve the text that prompts the user for input and displays the future value.
- Add blank lines to group the calculations.
- Align the numbers for each calculation.
- Allow the user to continue the program by entering only the single letter of "y" instead of having to enter all three letters of "yes".

Here, I decided to switch to Edit mode to apply changes directly to the Python file that's open in the code editor. This automatically added the Python file to the context for the prompt, which is what I wanted. Then, I entered the following prompt.

A prompt for improving the user interface

Can you modify the input and output so it looks like the following?

Future Value Calculator

Enter monthly investment: 100

Enter number of years: 3
Enter yearly interest rate: 3
Future value: 3771.46

Continue? (y/n): n

Bye!

Since the prompt doesn't use a mono-spaced font, you can't tell that I used spaces to align the numbers. To do that, I coded the prompt in a text editor that used a mono-spaced font. Then, I pasted it into the prompt.

When I sent this prompt to Copilot, it displayed the new code in the code editor in green and the old code in red. I accepted all changes and ran the program again to test whether the changes worked.

Based on the prompt, Copilot adjusted the code to allow the user to continue with a second calculation by entering "y", not "yes". I wasn't expecting that, but that's what I wanted, so I'm glad Copilot did that.

Unfortunately, the program still didn't format the output the way I wanted. When I ran the program, I got the following output.

A test run after the first prompt

```
Future Value Calculator
Enter monthly investment: 100
Enter number of years: 3
Enter yearly interest rate: 3
Future value: 3771.46
Continue? (y/n): n
Bye!
```

Since this didn't add the blank lines or alignment I was hoping for, I continued by entering the following prompt.

A prompt for fixing the blank lines

> That's pretty good, but can you add a blank line after the first line and before the "Continue" and "Bye!" lines?

The code changes looked right to me, so I accepted all changes and continued with another prompt.

A prompt for fixing the alignment

> The numbers input by the user don't align with the future value that's displayed. Can you align these numbers?

I accepted all changes and ran the program again. Then, I entered one calculation followed by "y" as shown next.

A test run after attempting to fix the blank lines and alignment

```
Future Value Calculator

Enter monthly investment: 100
Enter number of years: 3
Enter yearly interest rate: 3
Future value:               3771.46

Continue? (y/n): y
Enter monthly investment: 100
```

At this point, there were still a couple things I wanted to fix. I wanted to align the first two numbers with the second two numbers, and I wanted to add a blank line after the "Continue" prompt. So, I entered this prompt:

Another prompt for fixing the alignment

> The input for monthly investment and number of years doesn't align with the other two numbers (interest rate and future value). Can you align these numbers?

I accepted all changes and ran the program again, and the numbers were aligned correctly. However, the blank lines still weren't working exactly how I want, so I entered the following prompt.

Another prompt for the blank lines

> Can you remove the blank line from before the line that prints "Bye!" and add a blank line after the "Continue" prompt?

I accepted all changes and ran the program again. Then, I entered two calculations as shown next.

A test run after all improvements have been made

```
Future Value Calculator

Enter monthly investment:   100
Enter number of years:      1
Enter yearly interest rate: 0
Future value:               1200.00

Continue? (y/n): y

Enter monthly investment:   100
Enter number of years:      3
Enter yearly interest rate: 3
Future value:               3771.46
Continue? (y/n): n

Bye!
```

This time, it looked the way I wanted! Hooray!

At this point, I decided to pause development of this program. However, for a production program, I would consider using Copilot to improve this program. For example, Copilot can make it easy to generate a graphical user interface (GUI) for a program. So, I would consider using Copilot to generate a GUI for this program.

A review and a look forward

This chapter finishes by reviewing the prompts that I used to create the Python program. Then, it looks ahead by presenting some of the problems that you're likely to encounter with LLMs as you move forward.

The prompts for the Python program

Now that you understand some of the mechanics of using Copilot, let's take a moment to review the seven prompts that I used to create the Python program.

Prompt 1

Can you create a Python program that calculates the future value of a series of monthly payments over a specified number of years at a given interest rate?

Here are some specifications:

* Use the command line to get input and display output

* Get the monthly payment, years, and interest rate from the user.

* Use this input to calculate the future value.

* Allow the user to continue making calculations until the user chooses to end the program.

With this prompt, I tried to be specific and give Copilot all the information it needed to create the program I wanted. But I also tried to be concise, so I didn't have to type any extra info into the prompt.

One of the trickiest parts of writing a prompt is to enter the data that's needed without a lot of extra data. In this case, the prompt was good enough to get the program started, but it wasn't specific enough to generate the program exactly the way I wanted.

Prompt 2

> That's pretty good, but I'd like to use a loop to calculate the future value. Can you do that?

After reviewing the code generated by the first prompt, I asked Copilot to change the way the program calculated the future value. I did this because I knew that using a formula to calculate the future value might yield results that were different than the ones that I wanted.

I could have included this as part of the program specification, but when I was entering the first prompt, I thought Copilot might decide to use a loop without me having to prompt it to do that. Fortunately, it turned out to be easy to add this specification in the second prompt. That's because the chat already had a lot of context about the program, so this prompt didn't need to say much.

Prompt 3

> Can you modify the input and output so it looks like the following?
>
> Future Value Calculator
>
> Enter monthly investment: 100
> Enter number of years: 3
> Enter yearly interest rate: 3
> Future value: 3771.46
>
> Continue? (y/n): n
>
> Bye!

To reformat the input and output, I entered this prompt to provide an example of how I wanted the user interface to look, and Copilot was almost able to use this example to implement the interface, but not quite. So, I used the four prompts that follow to format the interface exactly how I wanted it.

Prompt 4

> That's pretty good, but can you add a blank line after the first line and before the "Continue" and "Bye!" lines?

Prompt 5

> The numbers input by the user don't align with the future value that's displayed. Can you align these numbers?

Prompt 6

> The input for monthly investment and number of years doesn't align with the other two numbers (interest rate and future value). Can you align these numbers?

Prompt 7

> Can you remove the blank line from before the line that prints "Bye!" and add a blank line after the "Continue" prompt?

In retrospect, I think I could have written these last four prompts better. If I could do it over, I would have started by focusing on inserting blank lines in the correct spots. Then, I would have turned my attention to aligning the numbers. Still, I was able to get the result I wanted, even if it wasn't the most efficient approach.

Overall, I was able to create the program that I wanted with just seven prompts. I think that's pretty amazing.

If you want to create the same Future Value program, you can use these prompts as a starting point. However, since LLMs are nondeterministic, you'll most likely need to modify these prompts as you go because the responses you get will be different than the ones that I got.

Problems with LLMs

When you work with an LLM, you may encounter the following problems.

Mistakes. By now, you already know that LLMs often make mistakes. Since an LLM can make things up that aren't real, this is sometimes known as *hallucinating*. With regard to programming, this means that an LLM can generate code that doesn't work the way you want or doesn't even run at all. As a result, you typically need to check the response given by an LLM to make sure it's accurate.

Copyright infringement. When you use an LLM to generate code, it may generate code that's identical to copyrighted code. This is rare, and it's difficult to avoid since you typically don't know what kinds of code Copilot's LLM was trained on or the details of how the model generates code. Generated code that matches copyrighted code is most likely to occur when there is little or no context for the prompt, or when the generated code represents a common approach. To identify and evaluate potential copyright infringement, many organizations employ code scanning policies.

Bias. An LLM may have biases in it due to biases in its training data. For example, if you ask an LLM to generate a drop-down list to select gender, it may generate a drop-down list that reflects biases that exist in the training data. Although the creators of an LLM can attempt to reduce bias in that LLM, this is a difficult task, and it may ultimately be impossible to completely eliminate bias from LLMs.

Cutoff date. An LLM has a cutoff date for its training data. As a result, after a version of an LLM is released, it doesn't receive any further training on new text or code that becomes available after its cutoff date. For software development, this poses challenges when you want to work with new features that were released after the LLM's cutoff date. To work around this issue, some AI assistants can add data to the context window by accessing the internet. However, if an AI assistant can't do that, it limits the assistant's ability to develop cutting-edge code.

Perspective

In this chapter, I avoided manually editing the generated code so I could focus on showing how to use Copilot to edit the code for you. To do that, I used the Chat window to generate and edit the code for the program. Depending on your level of programming experience, you may find that using the Chat window is more difficult than just writing the code yourself. In that case, you'll be glad to see that Copilot can also help you generate code by integrating into VS Code's code completion feature as described in the next chapter. Then, when you begin typing code, Copilot uses the context to suggest code completions that often do what you want.

Terms

artificial intelligence (AI)

machine learning (ML)

deep learning

generative AI

large language model (LLM)

natural language processing (NLP)

tokens

generative pretrained transformer (GPT)

AI assistant

AI agent

prompt

response

context

working memory

nondeterministic

deterministic

planning and reasoning systems

AI hallucination

Exercises

1. Create a web app that works like the Future Value web app presented in this chapter. To do that, you can start with the prompts presented in this chapter, but you'll most likely need to create your own prompts to finish this page.

2. Create a Python program that works like the Future Value program presented in this chapter. To do that, you can start with the prompts presented in this chapter, but you'll most likely need to create your own prompts to finish the program.

3. Add a graphical user interface (GUI) to the Future Value program presented in this chapter. To do that, you can start from the Future Value program that's available from the download for this book.

4. Create a web app that converts a temperature from Fahrenheit to Celsius.

5. Create a Python program that converts a temperature from Fahrenheit to Celsius.

Chapter 2

The essential skills for using Copilot

Now that you've seen how to use Copilot to develop a couple short programs, you're ready to learn the essential skills for using Copilot to generate and edit code. In addition, you're ready to learn some best practices for prompt engineering that apply to the LLMs that Copilot uses. Although this chapter uses Python for the code examples, the concepts and skills presented apply to all languages, and they should be easy enough to follow as long as you have a basic understanding of at least one programming language.

How to edit files **38**
Use the Chat window in Ask mode 38
Use the Chat window in Edit mode 40
Use the Chat window in Agent mode 42
Use inline chat...43
Use comment prompts 44
How to choose which technique to use..45

How to use chat participants and slash commands **47**
Use chat participants..47
Use slash commands 51

Best practices for prompt engineering... **54**
Be specific 54
Provide context..55
Specify output 55
Say what to do 55
Assign roles 56
Use structured formats...57

Types of prompts **58**
Zero-shot 58
Few-shot 58
Prompt chaining...59
Chain of thought..61
More types of prompts 62

Perspective... **63**

How to edit files

In the previous chapter, you learned how to use the Chat window to generate code in both Ask mode and Edit mode. Now, this chapter reviews those techniques and expands on them. In addition, it shows how Copilot can help you generate code directly in the code editor.

Use the Chat window in Ask mode

To open the Chat window, you can press Ctrl+Alt+I (Windows) or Cmd+Alt+I (macOS). Or, you can click on the Copilot icon at the top of the VS Code window as shown next.

The Copilot Icon

When you open the Chat window, it opens in Ask mode by default with your most recent chat for the current folder in the window. Then, when you enter a new prompt, Copilot uses the previous prompts and responses as the context for the chat. If you want to continue where you left off, that's usually what you want.

However, a long chat can increase the chances for Copilot to get confused and give weird or wrong answers. If that happens, you can start a new chat by clicking the New Chat (+) icon at the top of the Chat window as shown next.

The New Chat icon

When you have multiple chats within a folder, you can click on the Show Chats (clock) icon next to the New Chat icon as shown next.

The Show Chats icon

This displays the previous chats at the top of the VS Code window as shown next.

A new chat and an old chat

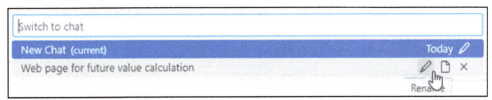

After you display the chats, you can click on the chat that you want to use. Or, you can organize your chats. To do that, you can click the Delete (x) icon to delete a chat you don't need anymore. Or, you can click the Rename (pencil) icon to rename a chat.

When Copilot suggests code in the Chat window, you can move the code into the code editor by clicking one of the three icons that appear when you hover over the suggested code. First, you can click the Apply icon to apply the suggested code to the file that's open in the code editor.

The Apply icon

```
def calculate_rectangle_area(width, height):
    """
```

Second, you can click the Insert At Cursor icon to insert the code at the cursor.

The Insert At Cursor icon

```
def calculate_rectangle_area(width, height):
    """
```

Third, you can click the Copy icon to copy the code to the clipboard, so you can paste it into the code editor later.

The Copy icon

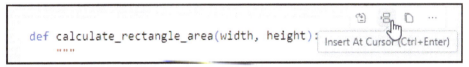

```
def calculate_rectangle_area(width, height):
    """
```

The fourth icon is a meatball menu icon (three dots) that opens a context menu with more options. These options let you insert the code into a Terminal window or into a new file.

Use the Chat window in Edit mode

If the Chat window is in Ask mode, you can switch to Edit mode by selecting Edit from the bottom of the prompt as shown next.

The menu for switching between Chat modes

When you switch between modes, Copilot warns you that this will end your current chat session. In other words, you'll lose the conversational context of the prompts and responses in the chat. That's because Ask and Edit modes function independently. However, you'll retain the context that's provided by the files that you're working on. So, you should only continue if you are OK with starting a new chat that uses your files as the context.

Most of the skills for working in Ask mode also apply to the Edit mode. For example, you may sometimes want to refresh the context for the Edit mode by starting a new chat. To do that, you can use the New Chat (+) icon just like you do when you're in Ask mode.

When you enter a prompt in Edit mode, Copilot writes the suggested code directly to the code editor. Then, the tab for the code editor displays a dot to indicate that it contains unsaved changes. In addition, the tab displays a square around the dot to indicate that Copilot's suggested changes haven't been accepted.

A code editor tab that contains unsaved Copilot changes

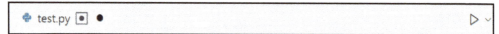

In the code editor, Copilot highlights suggested new code in green, and it highlights suggested deletions in red as shown next.

Suggested changes in the code editor

```
def calculate_square_area(side):                                    ✓ ? 🖫
def calculate_square_area(side_length):                             I
    """
    Calculate the area of a square.

    Parameters:
    side (float): The length of one side of the square.
    side_length (float): The length of one side of the square.

    Returns:
    float: The area of the square.
    """
    return side * side
    return side_length * side_length
```
Keep Undo 🖹 | 1 of 3 ↑ ↓ 🔗

To accept a change individually, you can hover the mouse over the change and click the Keep (check mark) icon that appears. Or, to accept all changes, you can click the Keep button that's displayed on the floating menu at the bottom of the editor.

You can also discard the suggested changes. To discard a change individually, you can hover the mouse over the change and click the Undo icon that appears. Or, to discard all changes, click the Undo button in the floating menu that's displayed at the bottom of the editor.

Even if you accept and save a change, you can still undo it later. To do that, switch to the Chat window and find the prompt for the change you want to undo. Then, click the Undo Requests (Delete) icon in the top right corner of the prompt as shown next.

Undo a request made by a prompt

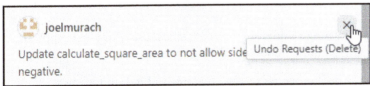

If you click the Undo Requests (Delete) icon, Copilot displays a dialog that asks if you really want to undo the edits. If you click Yes, Copilot undoes the changes made by the prompt and removes the prompt from the context.

This works similarly in Ask mode. However, since Ask mode doesn't automatically edit the code, undoing the request doesn't change the code.

Instead, it just removes the request from the context. This can be useful if you make a request that seems to confuse Copilot.

If you want Copilot to have code files as part of the context for a prompt, you need to provide them to the Chat window. By default, Copilot attaches the file that's currently open in the code editor to the prompt.

However, you can add more files to the prompt if you want. To add a single file, you can right-click on the file in the Explorer window and select Copilot ▶ Add File to Chat. To add multiple files, you can use the following procedure.

How to add multiple files to a prompt

1. Select the files in the Explorer window. To do that, you can hold down the Ctrl key and click on each file.
2. Right-click on the seleted files and select Copilot ▶ Add File to Chat. This adds all selected files to the prompt.

Use the Chat window in Agent mode

Besides the Chat and Edit modes, the Chat window also provides an Agent mode where Copilot acts as an agent that can perform tasks for you. Agent mode is similar to Edit mode in that it can edit code files for you. However, Agent mode also provides the following features.

Addition features provided by Agent mode

- Determines the context and files to edit automatically.
- Handles complex tasks that involve multiple steps.
- Starts tools and runs commands in the Terminal.
- Fixes problems in the generated code. To do that, it iterates multiple times to check whether the generated code works correctly and to fix any problems it detects.

However, these features come with the following drawbacks.

Drawbacks of Agent mode

- Takes longer to respond to your prompt. That's because it's doing more work for you.
- Causes you to reach your usage limits sooner. That's because a single prompt for a complex task may make many requests to the LLM.

At the time of this writing, Agent mode was a new feature, and it didn't always work as expected. However, with the rapid advances that Copilot has been making lately, it's likely to become more predictable and stable soon.

As a result, if you have a complex task, you should consider experimenting with Agent mode to see if it can handle your task. To do that, you can learn more by visiting the following URL. But first, we recommend learning how to use Ask and Edit modes.

A URL for learning more about Agent mode

https://code.visualstudio.com/docs/copilot/chat/chat-agent-mode

Use inline chat

If you don't want to use the Chat window, you can use the inline chat interface
to access Copilot from within the code editor. To do that, you can press Ctrl+I
(Windows) or Cmd+I (macOS). Then, Copilot displays a prompt within the
code editor as shown next.

An inline chat with a prompt that adds new code

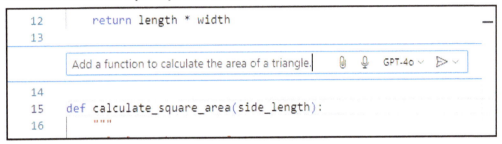

If you type the text for a prompt and press Enter, Copilot generates code and displays
suggested additions in green and suggested deletions, if any, in red as shown next.

The suggested new code in the code editor

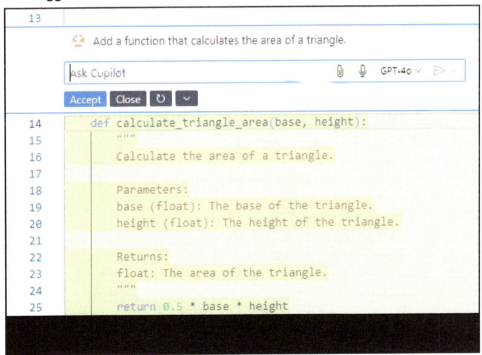

To accept the suggested new code, you can click the Accept button that's
displayed below the inline prompt.

You can also use the inline chat interface to modify code. To do that, use the following procedure to open the inline chat interface for the code you want to modify.

How to use the inline chat interface to modify code

3. Select the code you want to modify.
4. Click the Code Actions icon that appears to the left of the code. Or, press Ctrl+. (Windows) or Cmd+. (macOS).
5. Select "Modify using Copilot". This displays the inline chat interface.
6. Type your prompt and press Enter. This displays the suggested changes.
7. Accept or discard the suggested changes.

For instance, for the next example, I selected the line of code that returns the area of a rectangle. Then, I used the inline chat interface to enter a prompt that said, "Return -1 if the base or height is 0 or below." In response, it suggested the following code.

The suggested code modification in the code editor

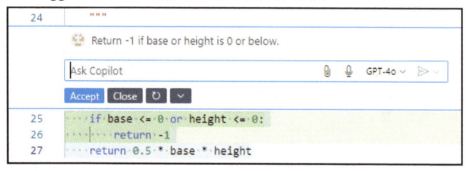

In this case, the suggested change did what I wanted, so I accepted it.

Use comment prompts

If you don't want to use the inline chat interface or the Chat window, you can use Copilot directly in the code editor. To do that, you can type comments or code, and Copilot generates code suggestions based on them. For example, to prompt Copilot for suggestions after entering a comment, you can press Enter. Then, to accept Copilot's suggestion, you can press Tab.

When using this technique, it's common to code a function signature and then describe the requirements for the function in a docstring comment. Sometimes, Copilot can guess what you want from the function signature and suggest the docstring comment for you!

In the following example, I started typing the signature of a function and Copilot guessed what I wanted from the context and suggested some comments and code in italics. This included the rest of the function signature, the docstring comment, and the function body. At this point, I clicked Tab to accept the suggested code.

A function signature with suggested code in italics

```
def calculate_circle_area(radius):
    """
    Calculate the area of a circle using the formula: pi * radius^2

    Parameters:
    radius (float): The radius of the circle

    Returns:
    float: The area of the circle
    """
    if radius <= 0:
        return -1
    return 3.14159 * radius**2
```

If you don't want to use docstring comments, you can use single-line comments as Copilot prompts. For instance, in the previous function, let's say I don't want to use the hard-coded value of 3.14159 for PI. Instead, I'd like to use the value for PI that's available from the Python math module.

Rather than regenerate all the code, I can enter the single-line comment shown here to prompt Copilot to import the math module.

A single line comment prompt

```
# import the math module
import math
```

Then, I can delete the code that uses the hard-coded value and use a single-line comment to generate code that uses the pi property as shown next.

Another single line comment prompt

```
# use math.pi to calculate the area of the circle
return math.pi * radius ** 2
```

When I enter the second comment prompt shown, I don't need to know whether the property for pi is named pi or PI. Instead, I can let Copilot figure that out for me.

How to choose which technique to use

Now that you've learned several ways to use Copilot to edit a code file, which one should you use? In general, that depends on personal preference and what you're trying to do, but here are a few thoughts on the subject.

The Chat window in Ask mode is useful when you don't yet know exactly how you want to proceed. You might start with a high-level prompt, such as "I'd like to create a tic-tac-toe game" and include some specs. Then you might continue to chat with Copilot to refine the code until you have a good starting point.

The Chat window in Edit mode is useful when you have some code that you want to edit. Then, you can use the code to provide context for the prompt, and use Edit mode to edit and refine the code.

The inline chat interface is useful when you're already in the code editor and you want to make small changes that aren't worth the effort of switching to the Chat window. That's especially true when you only want to modify selected code within a long code file.

Comment prompts are useful in a couple scenarios. First, single-line comments are useful if Copilot has generated code that's close to what you want, but you want to make some minor changes. In that case, you can delete the parts that aren't quite right and add single-line comments to guide Copilot toward the code you want.

Second, comment prompts are useful when it's easier to type the prompt in the code editor than it is to type the prompt in the Chat window. For instance, comment prompts are useful when you want to provide examples of what the output for a command line program should look like. That's because if you forget to press Shift-Enter for new lines, you could send the prompt to the LLM by accident by pressing Enter. In addition, when you type in the code editor, Copilot can make suggestions for the comment as well as the code.

For example, it's easier to type the following prompt as a comment in the code editor than as a prompt in the Chat window. In this example, after I typed the first line of asterisks in the code editor, Copilot suggested many of the subsequent lines of the comment, and I accepted them by pressing Tab. Similarly, Copilot suggested the parameters for the comment based on the function signature, and I accepted them by pressing Tab.

An instruction that's easier to type as a comment than as a prompt

```python
def print_shape_area(shape, area):
    """

    Print the area of a shape in this format:
    ********************************
    *            SHAPE AREA            *
    ********************************
    The area of the <shape> is: <area>
    ********************************


    Parameters:
    shape (str): The name of the shape.
    area (float): The area of the shape.
    """
```

By contrast, if I wanted to type this prompt in the Chat window, I'd need to type the entire prompt myself and press Shift+Enter after each line. In addition, since the Chat window doesn't use a monospaced font, it wouldn't show whether the characters in the prompt were aligned correctly.

How to use chat participants and slash commands

When you use Copilot from within VS Code, it provides a couple more tools to help you write prompts. A *chat participant* provides help with a certain subject area, and a *slash command* provides a shortcut to a common instruction. These tools are possible because GitHub Copilot provides an API that allows developers to extend the functionality of the Chat window by creating *chat extensions* such as chat participants.

Use chat participants

When you install the Copilot extension for VS Code, it provides several built-in chat participants. In addition, you can install other extensions for additional chat participants. To do that, you can get the extensions from either the VS Code Marketplace or the GitHub Marketplace.

To use a chat participant in the Chat window, you type @ in the prompt or click the @ symbol in the bottom left corner of the prompt window. When you do, Copilot displays a dialog that shows the available chat participants. Then, you can select the one you want to use.

Chat participants displayed above the prompt

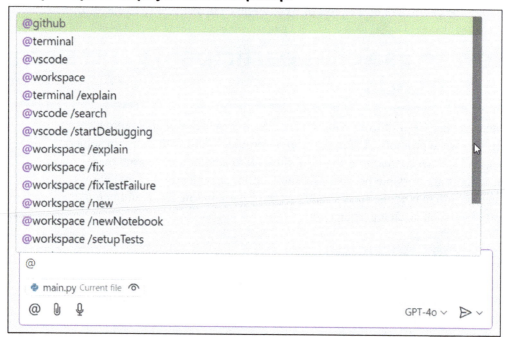

Here are the built-in chat participants, and their areas of expertise.

Built-in chat participants

Participant	Area of expertise
@workspace	The code in your workspace.
@vscode	The features of VS Code.
@terminal	The Terminal window that's integrated into VS Code.
@github	Working with GitHub or searching the web with Bing.

The following examples present some prompts that use chat participants, and the responses that they produced when I ran them.

A workspace prompt

@workspace what does the current file import?

A workspace response

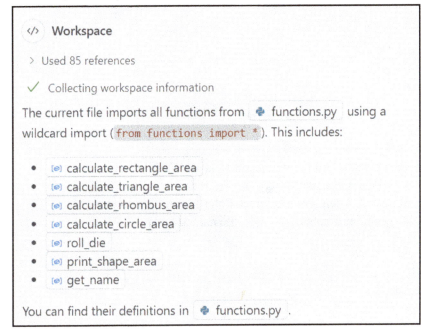

When I ran this prompt, I had a Python file open that imported all functions from another Python file named functions.py. So, this response provided a nice summary of these functions.

A VS Code prompt

@vscode can I float the Chat window?

A VS Code response

This response provides some useful information about opening a chat in a floating window instead of a window that's docked to the side of the VS Code window. In addition, you can click on the Show in Command Palette button to run the specified command.

A terminal prompt

@terminal how can I run the current file?

A terminal response

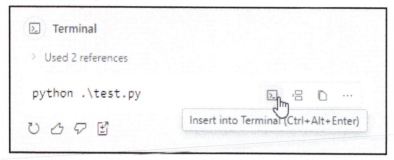

This response provides a command that you can run in VS Code's Terminal window. To do that, you can click the "Insert into Terminal" icon to insert the command into the Terminal. Then, you can press Enter to run the command. In this case, running the command runs the Python file named test.py that's in the current directory.

A GitHub prompt

@github list my repositories.

A GitHub response

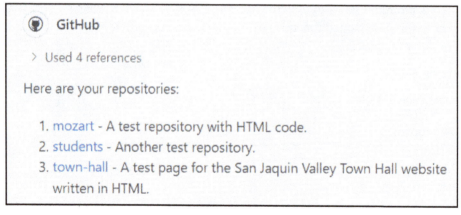

When I ran the GitHub prompt, I had to grant Copilot access to my repositories. Once I did that, it displayed my repositories in the response.

A GitHub prompt that uses #web to search the internet

@github #web did the Trailblazers win?

If you try to use #web to search the internet, it might not work on your system. That's because you need to have an account that supports this feature. Currently, you need to have a Microsoft 365 account or a Copilot Pro account.

However, if you have an account that supports this feature, Copilot will give you a response like the one that follows.

A GitHub response for a #web search

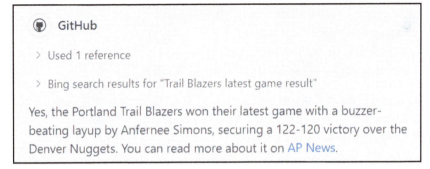

Use slash commands

When you use Copilot within VS Code, you can use several slash commands as shortcuts for common instructions. To use a slash command in the Chat window, you type a slash (/) in the input field. This displays the available slash commands. Then, you can select the one you want to use.

Available slash commands in the Chat window

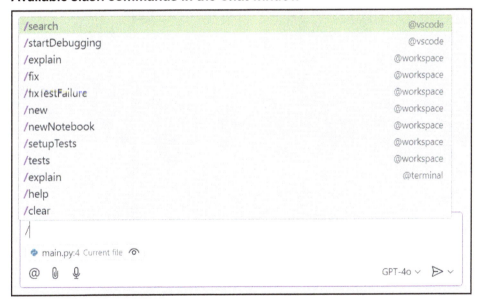

Here are some of the most common slash commands and what they do.

Common slash commands

Command	Description
/clear	Start a new chat session.
/help	Get information about how to use GitHub Copilot.
/explain	Explain how the selected code works.
/fix	Propose a fix for the problems in the selected code.
/new	Scaffold code for a new file or project in a workspace.

When you enter these commands, Copilot prefaces them with their chat participant when necessary. For example, if you enter the /explain command, Copilot prefaces it with the @workspace participant.

Here are some prompts that use slash commands, and the results that they produce.

The help command

/help

The help response

> 🐙 GitHub Copilot
>
> You can ask me general programming questions, or chat with the following participants which have specialized expertise and can perform actions:
>
> - @workspace - Ask about your workspace
>   - /explain - Explain how the code in your active editor works
>   - /tests - Generate unit tests for the selected code
>   - /fix - Propose a fix for the problems in the selected code
>   - /new - Scaffold code for a new file or project in a workspace
>   - /newNotebook - Create a new Jupyter Notebook
>   - /fixTestFailure - Propose a fix for the failing test
>   - /setupTests - Set up tests in your project (Experimental)
> - @vscode - Ask questions about VS Code
>   - /search - Generate query parameters for workspace search
>   - /startDebugging - Generate launch config and start debugging in VS Code (Experimental)
> - @terminal - Ask how to do something in the terminal
>   - /explain - Explain something in the terminal
> - @github - Get answers grounded in web search, code search, and your enterprise's knowledge bases

This response displays useful information about using Copilot's chat participants and slash commands.

Fix a function that doesn't handle negative values

@workspace /fix calculate_rectangle_area

The response for the fix

</> Workspace

> Used 1 reference

The [⊙] calculate_rectangle_area function calculates the area of a rectangle given its length and width. It returns the product of the length and width. If either the length or width is negative, it returns -1.

Here is the function with added validation to handle negative values:

This response also provides code for the suggested fix. You can review this code and determine whether it fixes the problem you were having. If it does, you can apply and accept this code.

Explain a function in the current file

@workspace /explain roll_die

The response with the explanation

</> Workspace

> Used 1 reference

The roll_die function is defined to simulate rolling a six-sided die. Here is the function from your file:

```python
def roll_die():
    return random.randint(1, 6)
```

This function uses the random.randint method to generate a random integer between 1 and 6, inclusive. Each call to roll_die will return a random number within this range, simulating the roll of a die.

To use this function, you need to import the random module at the top of your file:

```python
import random
```

This response provides a good explanation of a function named roll_die(), including information about a module that it depends on.

Best practices for prompt engineering

The goal of writing a prompt is to get the desired output from an LLM with minimal input. The art of prompt engineering is learning to understand what input the LLM needs to be able to generate the output you want. That requires creativity and good communication skills.

Be specific

When writing prompts, you should be specific. Your prompt shouldn't be too broad or include text that's unnecessary to get the desired response.

For example, if you want to create a Python program, the first prompt that follows isn't specific enough. The second prompt that follows is a little better and might be enough to get the program started. And the third prompt that follows is probably best since it provides the most specificity.

Poor - not specific enough

Can you calculate the future value of a series of monthly payments?

Better - more specific

Can you create a command-line Python program that calculates the future value of a series of monthly payments over a specified numbers of years at a given interest rate?

Best – most specific

Can you create a Python program that calculates the future value of a series of monthly payments over a specified number of years at a given interest rate?

Here are some specifications:
* Use the command line to get input and display output.
* Get the monthly payment, years, and interest rate from the user.
* Use this input to calculate the future value.
* Allow the user to continue making calculations until the user chooses to end the program.

Part of being specific is being precise. You should use clear, unambiguous language in your prompts.

Less precise

Get the required input from the user.

More precise

Get the monthly payment, years, and interest rate from the user.

Provide context

When writing prompts, you get better results if you provide *context*, or additional information that can help guide the LLM toward the results that you want.

Some examples of context

- The prompt
- Previous prompts and responses
- External files that you have added to the prompt

The *context window* refers to the amount of information, or context, that the LLM considers when it generates its response. Managing the context window can be tricky. That's because, in general, the more information you give the LLM, the more accurate its responses. But, too much information can confuse the LLM and lead to inaccurate or weird responses. With practice, you'll get a better feel for when to add more context, and when to start fresh with a new chat.

Specify output

One way to provide context for a prompt is to specify what the output should be. For instance, you can specify a range of values, or you can specify how a response should be formatted. This helps the LLM understand what you want.

Specify acceptable values

> Return a future value that's greater than zero.

Specify the format of the response

> Return a future value in this format:
> Future value: $<nnn>.<nn>

Say what to do

When prompting an LLM, it's better to tell it what to do than to tell it what not to do. That's because the LLM might struggle to figure out what you *do* want if you only tell it what you *don't* want. For instance, consider the two prompts that follow:

Poor – say what you don't want

> Don't use JavaScript to display the menu.

Good – say what you do want

> Use CSS to display the menu.

With the first prompt, the LLM has to guess how to display the menu and it may not guess what you want. With the second prompt, the LLM knows what language you want to use to display the menu.

Another problem with telling an LLM what not to do is it can be hard to think of all the things you want to avoid. For instance, if you're generating a paragraph of text and you say "No jargon" and "No swearing", does that mean you're OK with racist material? The LLM doesn't know.

It's better to specify what you want the response to include. This is also called *constraint-based prompting*. The following table summarizes some of the constraints that you can include in a prompt.

Types of constraints

Constraint	Description
Format constraint	Require a specific structure, such as JSON, a list of objects, a table of data, and so on.
Length constraint	Require a maximum word count, a specific line count, a maximum length of a line, a specific number of paragraphs, and so on.
Style constraint	Require a specific tone, such as non-technical or scientific.
Content constraint	Require the content to contain specific information.
Role-based constraint	Assign roles to the LLM as described in the next heading.

When specifying output, it's OK to say what you don't want, as long as you combine it with what you do want as shown next.

Combine what you want with what you don't want

> Generate two paragraphs that explain the future value program. Tone should be friendly and conversational – no jargon.

Assign roles

You can assign roles to the LLM and to the intended audience in your prompts. The roles help the LLM shape its response to accommodate the perspective or expertise of the stated role.

Assign a role to the LLM

> You are an experienced Python developer. Generate a function that calculates the future value of a series of monthly payments over a specified numbers of years at a given interest rate.

Assign a role to the LLM and to the intended audience

> You are an experienced Python programmer and trainer. Generate a function that calculates a future value. Make sure the code is easy for a beginning programmer to understand.

Use structured formats

When you write a prompt for an LLM, it can be useful to use labels and delimiters to structure the prompts. That way, it's clear to the LLM what part of the prompt is instruction and what part is context. When you use this technique, the instruction should come first, followed by any relevant context.

A prompt that uses labels

Instruction: create a Python program that calculates the future value of a series of monthly payments over a specified number of years at a given interest rate.

Specifications:
* Use the command line to get input and display output.
* Get the monthly payment, years, and interest rate from the user.
* Use this input to calculate the future value.
* Allow the user to continue making calculations until the user chooses to end the program.

Output: decimal number rounded to 2 digits.

Output display format: Future Value: $<nnn>.<nn>

A prompt that uses labels and delimiters

Instruction:
Create a Python program that calculates the future value of a series of monthly payments over a specified number of years at a given interest rate.

Specifications:
* Use the command line to get input and display output.
* Get the monthly payment, years, and interest rate from the user.
* Use this input to calculate the future value.
* Allow the user to continue making calculations until the user chooses to end the program.

Output:
Type: decimal number rounded to 2 digits.
Display format:: Future Value: $<nnn>.<nn>

You can also use this technique when you enter comment prompts. Formatting comment prompts like this has the added benefit of documenting the code for other programmers and for your future self.

Types of prompts

Now that you know some of the best practices for writing prompts, you're ready to learn some common types of prompts. Since this book has already shown examples of some of these types of prompts, some of this content is review.

Zero-shot

A *zero-shot prompt* contains no additional information. Instead, it relies on the LLM's training data.

A zero-shot prompt for a list

> Generate a list of the 50 states in the USA and their capitals.

A zero-shot prompt for a function

> Generate a Python function that calculates the area of a circle.

When there's a good chance that the LLM's training data is adequate to provide a good response, a zero-shot prompt can work. For instance, the two previous prompts are good candidates for zero-shot prompts because you probably don't need much context to generate a list of states or a function for the area of a circle.

Few-shot

A *few-shot prompt* contains one or more examples to help guide the LLM toward the result that you want. A few-shot prompt that contains only one example is also called a *one-shot prompt*.

The examples provide the LLM with information on desired input and output, and can also tell the LLM how to handle special cases, missing data, or edge cases.

A few-shot prompt

> ### Task:
> Create a Python function that accepts a date of birth and optional date of death and calculates age. If no date of death, use current date.
>
> ### Examples:
> # Example 1
> Input: 6/5/1957
> Output: 67
>
> # Example 2
> Input: 6/5/1957, 12/22/2010
> Output: 53

```
# Example 3
Input:
Output: throw ValueError

# Example 4
Input: 10 years ago
Output: throw ValueError

# Example 5
Input: 6/5/1657
Output: throw ValueError
```

In this prompt, the first example shows the expected output when the function receives a date of birth only, while the second shows the expected output when the function receives both a date of birth and a date of death. The third example shows how to handle missing input, the fourth shows how to handle input that isn't a date, and the fifth shows how to handle a date of birth that's too far in the past. Here, the last three examples let the LLM know that it should throw an error when it receives invalid or missing data.

Prompt chaining

Prompt chaining uses multiple prompts to produce a result, with subsequent prompts building on earlier ones. This allows you to have a conversation with an LLM to shape the output.

Chapter 1 used this technique to create the Future Value program. In the response to the first prompt, Copilot generated some code that included a function to calculate a future value. Then, the second prompt requested a change in the function that calculates the future value. Copilot used the first prompt and its response as context for this second prompt. And the rest of the prompts continued the conversation to finish creating the program.

Prompt chaining also allows you to break a complex task into subtasks. Then, you can prompt the LLM one subtask at a time, and the LLM uses the earlier prompts and responses as context for subsequent prompts. For example, the three prompts that follow break a complex task into three subtasks.

Prompt #1

```
### Task: Create a Python function that calculates the future value of a series of
monthly payments over a specified numbers of years at a given interest rate.
```

This prompt creates a function that calculates a future value. Once you're satisfied with the result, you can move on to the next subtask.

Prompt #2

> ### Task: Create a Python function that accepts a list with monthly payment amount, number of years, and annual interest rate and calls the calculate_future_value function for each item in the list.
>
> ### list example:
> ```
> [
>   {
>       "amount": 100,
>       "years": 10,
>       "interest": 0.4
>   },
>   ...
> ]
> ```

This prompt creates a function that accepts some data and uses that data to call the function created in the first prompt. Note that the second prompt provides context about the data that the function accepts.

Prompt #3

> ### Task: Create a main function that creates a list of 5 items, passes the list to the process_future_values function, and displays the results in the Terminal.
>
> ### Output format:
> <BLANKLINE>
> Monthly payment: <amount>
> Number of years: <years>
> Interest rate: <interest>
> ~~~~~~~~~~~~~~~~~~~~~~~~~~~~
> Future value: <fv>
> <BLANKLINE>

This prompt creates a main() function that generates some data, sends it to the function created in the second prompt, and displays the return data in the Terminal. Since the third prompt has access to the context from the earlier prompts, it doesn't need to provide context about the data to send to the function.

By contrast, the third prompt does provide context about what the output to the terminal should look like. To do that, it uses <BLANKLINE> to represent a blank line, and it uses placeholders like <amount> and <years> to indicate the data returned by the function.

Instead of using prompt chaining, you could try to prompt the LLM to create all of this code at once, and it might be able to generate all three functions adequately. However, asking the LLM to perform multiple tasks at once increases the chances of the LLM getting confused. By breaking a task into subtasks, you increase the chances of getting the result you want. Another benefit is that you can adjust the code that the LLM generates for each subtask before continuing with the next subtask. This provides a better context for the next subtask, which increases the chances of getting the result you want.

Chain of thought

Recently, there have been many advances in reasoning systems that AI uses for questions involving math, science, and computer programming. As a result, AI systems are getting better at reasoning. However, if an AI system is struggling with prompts that ask it to reason, you can sometimes use *chain of thought prompting* to encourage an LLM to "think out loud" or to "show its work".

For example, the following prompt provides an example question and answer to show the LLM how it should break the task into steps and show its work.

A chain-of thought prompt

Q. Maisie has 5 cards. She draws 1 card of each suit. How many cards does she have?

A. Maisie started with 5 cards. There are 4 suits in a deck of cards. Maisie drew one of each suit, 5+1+1+1+1. The answer is 9.

Q. I received 4 scented candles for Christmas. I re-gifted 2 of them for New Years. Then I received another scented candle for Valentine's Day. How many scented candles do I have?

A.

You can also create a chain-of-thought prompt by describing the reasoning steps the LLM should use as shown next.

Another chain-of-thought prompt

Create a Python function that calculates the future value of a monthly investment based on years and interest. Within the function, break it down step by step:

First, convert the annual interest rate to a monthly interest rate.

Second, calculate the total number of months.

Third, calculate the future value.

Both of the previous chain-of-thought prompts explain the steps the LLM should take. However, that's not always necessary. Sometimes, you only need to tell an LLM to show its work. This can be as simple as adding a phrase like "Let's think step by step" to your prompt. This is sometimes called a *zero-shot chain-of-thought prompt* because you don't provide examples.

A zero-shot chain-of-thought prompt

> Q. I have 16 balls. Half of the balls are golf balls, and 3/4 of the golf balls are green. How many green balls do I have?
> A. Let's think step by step.

Many LLMs are starting to return step-by-step results without being prompted to. For instance, when I entered the previous prompt into Copilot and ChatGPT without "Let's think step by step" in the prompt, they both still described the steps they took to arrive at the answer, rather than just presenting the answer. And, they both arrived at the correct answer!

Chain of thought prompting can improve accuracy and provide transparency by making it easier to see how an LLM arrived at its answer and, if there are problems, where it might have gone wrong. Unfortunately, recent research suggests that an LLM's explanation of the steps it took to reach its answer can be misleading. As a result, while chain of thought prompting can be helpful, you can't always trust what an LLM reports about its reasoning.

More types of prompts

The types of prompts presented here should be enough to get you off to a good start with prompt engineering. However, there are some other types of prompts that you may run across as you learn more about prompt engineering. Here's a brief description of some of them.

Self-consistency sampling. Run the same prompt multiple times to generate multiple responses. Then, compare the responses and choose the most consistent one.

Tree-of-thought prompting. Break a task down into smaller steps. Then, explore the steps, like the branches of a tree. This is useful for complex tasks or extended reasoning.

Retrieval augmented generation (RAG). Let an LLM access external data or documents to complete a task. This can overcome issues like knowledge limits or date cutoffs in training data.

Fine tuning. Technically, this isn't a type of prompt. Rather, you use fine tuning to take a pre-trained model and adapt it to a specific task by training it further on a smaller, task-specific dataset. This refines the LLMs capabilities and improves its accuracy, which makes it easier to prompt successfully.

Perspective

This chapter presented the essential skills for using Copilot to generate and edit code. In addition, it presented some best practices for prompt engineering that apply to the LLMs that Copilot uses. At this point, you have the skills you need to start using Copilot to develop software. However, there's always more to learn. That's why the chapters in the next section present some additional strategies and skills.

Terms

chat participant

slash command

chat extension

context

context window

constraint-based prompting

zero-shot prompt

few-shot prompt

one-shot prompt

prompt chaining

chain of thought prompting

zero-shot chain-of-thought prompt

Exercises

Use the any of the skills presented in this chapter to perform the following tasks as easily and efficiently as possible.

1. Create a Python file named shapes.py and generate functions that calculate the area of a square, a rectangle, a triangle, and a circle. Also, generate a function that calculates the circumference of a circle.
2. Create a web app that calculates the area and circumference of a circle based on the radius of a circle.
3. Create a Python program that calculates the area and circumference of a circle based on the radius of the circle.

Section 2

More skills as you need them

Section 1 presented a subset of the skills for using Copilot to generate and modify code. Now, this section reviews some of these skills and presents more Copilot skills that you can learn whenever you need them. To make that possible, each chapter in this section has been written as an independent module. As a result, you can read these chapters in whatever sequence you prefer.

Chapter 3

Create a Python program

Chapter 1 showed how to use Copilot to create a short Python program. Now, this chapter shows how to use Copilot to help you create a longer Python program that allows two people to play a dice game known as Pig. Along the way, it illustrates several techniques that you can use to handle typical issues that arise when using Copilot to create significant programs.

Since Copilot makes mistakes, testing the code that it generates is critical. That's why this chapter begins by showing how to use Python doctests to automate testing. That way, you can quickly test code generated by Copilot to make sure it works correctly.

How to use Python doctests with Copilot..**68**
How to add a doctest to a function 68
How to run doctests 69
How to use Copilot to write doctests..70
How to simulate user input or random numbers 71

Generate the initial code..**74**
Make a plan in the Chat window 74
Apply the code to the files 77
Run the program 78
Run the doctests..79

Improve the initial code..**82**
Add a graphical representation of a die...82
Format the player scores 87
Format the player turn...90

Refactor the code..**94**
Ask Copilot for advice 94
Convert from functions to objects 94
Run the program 97

Perspective...**98**

How to use Python doctests with Copilot

When you code a function in Python, it can be useful to include a *doctest*, which is a simple automated test that's stored in a docstring comment at the beginning of the function. Then, you can run the doctest in the Terminal window, and it can help you identify problems with a function. As an added benefit, adding a doctest to the beginning of a function can guide Copilot in generating the code for the rest of the function.

Although doctests provide a good starting point for automating testing, it's generally considered a good practice to use a technique known as *unit testing* to provide more complete automated testing. That's why chapter 7 explains unit testing in more detail. But, for now, you can use doctests to perform some simple tests and help Copilot understand what a function should do.

This chapter shows how to get started with doctests. However, it doesn't present the details of the syntax for working with them because Copilot can handle those details for you!

How to add a doctest to a function

To add a doctest to a function, you start by adding a docstring comment. Within the docstring, you add a line that starts with >>> followed by any Python code that you want to execute for testing. Typically, this includes a call to the function that's being tested.

After the call to the function, you enter the result you expect from the function. The expected results are *not* preceded with >>>.

The following example shows two doctests in a function that calculates the area of a triangle. The first tests the function by passing it valid values, and the second tests the function by passing it an invalid value. Here, the test for the invalid value indicates that the function should return -1 if either argument is a negative value.

A function with two doctests

```
def calculate_triangle_area(base, height):
    """
    Doctests:
    >>> calculate_triangle_area(5, 10)
    25.0
    >>> calculate_triangle_area(-1, 10)
    -1
    """
    if base <= 0 or height <= 0:
        return -1
    return (base * height) / 2
```

How to run doctests

Before you can run the doctests, you must import the doctest module in the file that contains the doctests. Then, you call the testmod() function as shown in the following example.

Code that imports the doctest module and runs the doctests

```
if __name__ == "__main__":
    import doctest
    doctest.testmod()
```

After you add this code to a file, you can run doctests by running the file. If the tests pass, the Terminal doesn't display any messages as shown next.

The Terminal when the tests pass

```
PS C:\murach\ai\ch3\doctests> & C:/Users/maryd/AppData/Local/Programs/
Python/Python313/python.exe c:/murach/ai/ch3/doctests/main.py
PS C:\murach\ai\ch3\doctests>
```

However, if any test fails, the Terminal displays information about the tests that failed. For example, if you removed the if statement from the previous function, one doctest would fail. Then, the Terminal would display the following info.

The Terminal when a test fails

```
PS C:\murach\ai\ch3\doctests> & C:/Users/maryd/AppData/Local/Programs/
Python/Python313/python.exe c:/murach/ai/ch3/doctests/main.py
***********************************************************************
File "c:\murach\ai\ch3\doctests\main.py", line 15, in __main__.calcula
te_triangle_area
Failed example:
    calculate_triangle_area(-1, 10)
Expected:
    -1
Got:
    -5.0
***********************************************************************
1 item had failures:
   1 of   2 in __main__.calculate_triangle_area
***Test Failed*** 1 failure.
PS C:\murach\ai\ch3\doctests>
```

This info shows that the second test failed because the function call returns a value of -5.0, and the doctest expected it to return a value of -1.

Sometimes you may want more info about the tests, even when they pass. For instance, after you create the tests for the first time, you might want to see all of the tests in the Terminal to make sure they're running. To do that, you can run the testmod() method with verbose output as shown next.

The testmod() method with verbose output

```
doctest.testmod(verbose=True)
```

Then, when you run the doctests, you'll get more detailed info as shown next.

The Terminal with verbose output

```
PS C:\murach\ai\ch3\doctests> & C:/Users/maryd/AppData/Local/Programs/
Python/Python313/python.exe c:/murach/ai/ch3/doctests/main.py
Trying:
    calculate_triangle_area(5, 10)
Expecting:
    25.0
ok
Trying:
    calculate_triangle_area(-1, 10)
Expecting:
    -1
ok
3 items had no tests:
    __main__
    __main__.calculate_circle_area
    __main__.calculate_rectangle_area
1 item passed all tests:
    2 tests in __main__.calculate_triangle_area
2 tests in 4 items.
2 passed.
Test passed.
PS C:\murach\ai\ch3\doctests>
```

This shows that both tests in the calculate_triangle_area() function ran and passed. It also shows that there are three other functions in the main.py file that don't have any tests yet.

How to use Copilot to write doctests

It's easy to use Copilot to generate the doctests for you. For example, you can add a new function and its doctests by entering a prompt like this:

A prompt that adds a new function and its doctests

Add a function that calculates the area of a rhombus. Include doctests.

When you do that, Copilot uses the other doctests in the file as context and generates doctests for the new function like these:

The two doctests for the function

```
>>> calculate_rhombus_area(5, 10)
25.0
>>> calculate_rhombus_area(-1, 10)
-1
```

If the doctests that Copilot generates aren't what you want, you can use the Chat window in Edit mode or the inline chat interface to change them.

If a function doesn't contain any doctests, you can use the Chat window in Edit mode or the inline chat interface to add them. For example, you can use the following prompt to add doctests to an existing function.

A prompt that adds doctests to an existing function

In the calculate_circle_area() function, add doctests that test a valid value and an invalid value.

Sometimes Copilot generates the doctests you ask for but doesn't generate the code to run them. In that case, you can use a prompt like the following one to add the necessary code.

A prompt that adds code to run the doctests

Add code to run the doctests.

Or, if you want more info about the tests, you can use a prompt like the following one.

A prompt for getting more info when running the doctests

Add code to run the doctests with verbose output.

How to simulate user input or random numbers

If a function you want to test uses the input() function to get input from the user, you want to be able to specify the value a user entered without having to manually enter a value in the Terminal. Similarly, if a function you're testing uses a random number, you want to be able to specify the "random" number so your doctest knows what to expect.

There are several ways to do this in Python, but one common technique is to use the patch() function of the unittest.mock module. Since Copilot can usually implement this technique for you, you don't need to know the syntax of the patch() function to use it. For example, let's say you have the following function that asks the user for input.

A function that asks the user for input

```
def get_name():
    return input("What is your name? ")
```

For this function, you can use the following prompt to generate a doctest that uses the patch() function.

A prompt that instructs Copilot to use the patch() function

Add doctests to the get_name() function. Use the patch function to simulate user input.

When I entered this prompt, Copilot generated the following doctest.

The doctest that Copilot generated

```
>>> from unittest.mock import patch
>>> with patch('builtins.input', return_value='Alice'):
...     get_name()
'Alice'
```

This doctest begins by importing the patch() function from the unittest.mock module. Then, it uses the patch() function to return a string of "Alice" for the first input prompt in the get_name() function.

You can use a similar technique to simulate the testing of a random number. For example, let's say you want Copilot to generate a function named roll_die() that returns a random integer from 1 to 6. In that case, you enter a prompt like the one shown next to have Copilot generate the function and doctests that use the patch() function.

Another prompt that instructs Copilot to use the patch() function

Add a roll_die() function. Include doctests that use the patch() function to simulate die rolls.

When I entered this prompt, Copilot generated the following function and doctests.

The function and doctests that Copilot generated

```
def roll_die():
    """
    Simulate rolling a six-sided die.

    Returns:
    int: The result of the die roll (1-6).

    Doctests:
    >>> from unittest.mock import patch
    >>> with patch('random.randint', return_value=3):
    ...     roll_die()
    3
    >>> with patch('random.randint', return_value=6):
    ...     roll_die()
```

```
6
«»»
return random.randint(1, 6)
```

In these two doctests, the first simulates when the roll_die() function returns a 3, and the second simulates when the roll_die() function returns a 6.

Sometimes Copilot generates doctests that fail. When that happens, you can ask Copilot to explain the code in the doctest. That can help you figure out how to make the doctest pass.

A simple way to ask Copilot to explain code

1. Select the code in the code editor.
2. Right+click (Windows) or Ctrl+click (macOS) the selected code. This displays a context menu.
3. Select Copilot ▶ Explain.

Selecting Copilot ▶ Explain opens the Chat window and automatically enters a prompt like the one shown next. This prompt uses the @workspace chat participant and the /explain slash command.

A prompt for an explanation in the Chat window

```
@workspace /explain Write an explanation for the active selection as paragraphs of text.

>>> from unittest.mock import patch
    >>> with patch('random.randint', return_value=3):
    ...     roll_die()
```

After the prompt, the Chat window provides an explanation of the selected code. For example, the following Chat window explains the use of the patch() function in the first doctest for the roll_die() function.

An explanation in the Chat window

</> Workspace

> Used 1 reference

The provided code snippet demonstrates the use of the `unittest.mock` module to temporarily replace the behavior of the `random.randint` function. This is useful in unit testing when you want to control the output of functions that produce random or non-deterministic results.

The `from unittest.mock import patch` statement imports the `patch` function from the `unittest.mock` module. The `patch` function is used to replace the specified target with a mock object during the scope of a `with` statement.

In the `with patch('random.randint', return_value=3):` line, the `patch` function is used to replace the `random.randint` function with a mock that always returns the value `3`. This means that any call to `random.randint` within the `with` block will return `3` instead of a random integer.

Inside the `with` block, the `roll_die()` function is called. Although the implementation of `roll_die()` is not provided, we can infer that it likely calls `random.randint` to simulate rolling a die. By patching `random.randint` to always return `3`, the test ensures that `roll_die()` will behave as if the die always rolls a three, allowing for predictable and repeatable test results.

This technique is particularly useful in unit tests to ensure that tests are not affected by random variations and can reliably test the behavior of the code under specific conditions.

Generate the initial code

To start the Pig program, I created a folder named pig. Then, I used VS Code to open this folder and to create two blank Python files named pigdice.py and main.py. I did this because I wanted the pigdice.py file to contain the functions for the game as well as some doctests for those functions. And, I wanted the main.py file to contain the main() function that runs the game by calling functions from the pigdice.py file.

Make a plan in the Chat window

After creating the files for the program, I opened the Chat window. By default, it was in Ask mode, which is what I wanted. So, I entered the following prompt. In general terms, this prompt describes what I want the program to do and provides some specifications for the program. It also asks Copilot for feedback, in case there was anything I missed or should consider.

The initial prompt in the Chat window

Task:
Create a basic 2-person command-line Pig dice game.

```
### Specs:
# Players should be named Player 1 and Player 2
# Game should end when a player reaches 20 points

### Files:
# pigdice.py
  * Contains the functions for the game
  * Each function should have at least one doctest
# main.py
  * Contains the main function that runs the game.
  * The main function should...
      * Display a message that says "Let's play Pig!"
      * Display the rules of the game
      * Continue playing the game until it ends
      * Display "Thanks for playing!" when the game ends

Do you have any questions about these specifications or suggestions for other
features/functionality?
```

Copilot responded that it didn't have any questions and generated proposed
code for the two files.

The proposed code for the pigdice.py file

```python
import random

def display_rules():
    """
    Display the rules of the Pig dice game.

    >>> display_rules()
    # Copilot generated 10 lines of expected results - NOT SHOWN HERE #
    """
    print("Pig Dice Game Rules:")
    print("1. The game is played by two players: Player 1 and Player 2.")
    print("2. Players take turns to roll a die as many times as they wish...")
    print("3. If a player rolls a 1, they score nothing for that turn and...")
    print("4. A player can choose to hold (stop rolling) to add their...")
    print("5. The first player to reach or exceed 20 points wins the game.")

def roll_die():
    """
    Roll a six-sided die and return the result.

    >>> result = roll_die()
    >>> 1 <= result <= 6
    True
    """
    return random.randint(1, 6)

def play_turn(player):
    """
    Play a single turn for the given player.

    Args:
        player (str): The name of the player ("Player 1" or "Player 2").
```

```
    Returns:
        int: The total points scored by the player in this turn.

    >>> random.seed(0)
    >>> play_turn("Player 1")
    Player 1 rolled a 4
    Player 1 rolled a 4
    Player 1 rolled a 1
    Player 1's turn total is 0
    0
    """
    turn_total = 0
    while True:
        roll = roll_die()
        print(f"{player} rolled a {roll}")
        if roll == 1:
            turn_total = 0
            break
        turn_total += roll
        if input(f"{player}, do you want to roll again? (y/n) ").lower() != 'y':
            break
    print(f"{player}'s turn total is {turn_total}")
    return turn_total

def play_game():
    """
    Play a game of Pig between Player 1 and Player 2.
    Returns:
        bool: True if the game should be played again,
        False otherwise.

    >>> random.seed(0)
    >>> play_game()
    # Copilot generated 71 lines of expected results - NOT SHOWN HERE#
    """
    display_rules()
    scores = {"Player 1": 0, "Player 2": 0}
    while scores["Player 1"] < 20 and scores["Player 2"] < 20:
        for player in ["Player 1", "Player 2"]:
            scores[player] += play_turn(player)
            print(f"Player 1's score: {scores['Player 1']}")
            print(f"Player 2's score: {scores['Player 2']}")
            if scores[player] >= 20:
                print(f"{player} wins!")
                return input("Do you want to play again? (y/n) ").lower() == 'y'
    return False
```

The proposed code for the main.py file

```
from pigdice import play_game

def main():
    print("Let's play Pig!")
    while play_game():
        pass
    print("Thanks for playing!")

if __name__ == "__main__":
    main()
```

At this point, I read through this code and thought that it seemed like a reasonable starting point. However, I noticed a few issues that I wanted to fix.

First, the play_game() function starts by calling the display_rules() function. However, I want the program to display the rules once when the program starts, not after every game.

Second, I thought the doctests for the display_rules() and play_game() functions were too long, which is why the previous code listing doesn't show them. I also thought they were unnecessary. That's because the doctest for display_rules() was so simple that it wasn't helpful, and the doctest for play_game() was too complex to be useful. So, I decided to remove these doctests from both functions.

Third, the doctest for the play_turn() function didn't seem like it would pass. When I read the code, I didn't see how passing 0 to the seed() method could produce 4 twice and then 1. In addition, the doctest didn't handle user input. However, since the code for the function looked good, I decided not to worry about the doctest just yet. Instead, I decided to fix it later.

To address the other issues, I entered a follow-up prompt in the Chat window as shown next.

The follow-up prompt in the Chat window

> That's a good start, but I'd like to change a couple things:
>
> * I think the doctest in display_rules is too simple and the doctest in play_game is too long/complex. Please remove them both.
>
> * I don't want to display the rules after every game. I just want to display them once, when the program starts.

When I entered this prompt, Copilot made the requested changes to the proposed code and displayed them in the Chat window.

Apply the code to the files

I was satisfied with the changes that Copilot made, so I used the Apply icon to write that code to the program files.

Apply the proposed code to pigdice.py

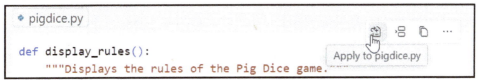

Apply the proposed code to main.py

```
◆ main.py                                        ⌨  ⊟  ⎘  ⋯

  from pigdice import display_rules, play_game    ┌──────────────────┐
                                                   │ Apply to main.py │
                                                   └──────────────────┘
  def main():
```

Run the program

After applying the changes and saving the files, I ran the code in main.py to play the game. This displayed the game in the Terminal as shown next.

The game in the Terminal

```
Let's Play Pig!
Pig Dice Game Rules:
1. The game is played by two players: Player 1 and Player 2.
2. Players take turns to roll a die as many times as they wish, adding the rolled
value to a turn total.
3. If a player rolls a 1, they score nothing for that turn and it becomes the next
player's turn.
4. A player can choose to hold (stop rolling) to add their turn total to their score.
5. The first player to reach or exceed 20 points wins the game.
Player 1 rolled a 3
Player 1, do you want to roll again? (y/n) y
Player 1 rolled a 2
Player 1, do you want to roll again? (y/n) n
Player 1's turn total is 5
Player 1's score: 5
Player 2's score: 0
Player 2 rolled a 6
Player 2, do you want to roll again? (y/n) y
Player 2 rolled a 6
Player 2, do you want to roll again? (y/n) n
Player 2's turn total is 12
Player 1's score: 5
Player 2's score: 12
Player 1 rolled a 2
Player 1, do you want to roll again? (y/n) y
Player 1 rolled a 1
Player 1's turn total is 0
Player 1's score: 5
Player 2's score: 12
Player 2 rolled a 6
Player 2, do you want to roll again? (y/n)
```

As I played the game, I was pleased to find that it behaved as expected. In other words, it let two people play a game of Pig. However, I made a mental note that I would like to improve the formatting for the user interface to make it easier to read.

Run the doctests

Before working on any improvements, I wanted to run the doctests in the pigdice.py file and make sure they all pass. Since Copilot didn't include any code to run the tests, I needed to add that first.

To do that, I decided to use the Chat window in Edit mode. So, I made sure to switch to Edit mode by selecting Edit from the drop-down list at the bottom of the prompt. Then, I added both Python files to the prompt and entered the following text.

The prompt in the Chat window

> Please add code to pigdice.py to run the doctests with verbose output.

In response, Copilot added an import statement to the top of the pigdice.py file and code to run the tests to the bottom of the file. I accepted both changes and saved the file. Then, I ran the pigdice.py file, which ran the doctests. When I did, the test in the roll_die() function passed. But, as expected, the test in the play_turn() function failed with the following info.

Failure info for the play_turn test

```
**************************************************************
File "c:\murach\ai\ch3\pig\pigdice.py", line 37, in __main__.play_turn
Failed example:
    play_turn("Player 1")
Expected:
    Player 1 rolled a 4
    Player 1 rolled a 4
    Player 1 rolled a 1
    Player 1's turn total is 0

    0
Got:
    Player 1 rolled a 4
    Player 1, do you want to roll again? (y/n) Player 1's turn total is 4
    4
```

To fix this doctest, I used the next prompt to ask Copilot to use the patch() function to simulate user input and random numbers. I also specified that I wanted it to include tests for when the user rolls a 1 and when they choose not to roll again.

The prompt in the Chat window to fix the failing doctest

> ### Task: Update the doctests for play_turn() to use the patch function to simulate user input and set the random number returned by roll_die().
>
> ### Specs: Test when the user rolls a 1 and when they choose not to roll again.

The doctests that Copilot generated

```
>>> from unittest.mock import patch
>>> with patch('builtins.input', side_effect=['y', 'n']):
...     with patch('random.randint', side_effect=[5, 6, 1]):
...         play_turn("Player 1")
Player 1 rolled a 5
Player 1 rolled a 6
Player 1 rolled a 1
Player 1's turn total is 0
0
>>> with patch('builtins.input', side_effect=['n']):
...     with patch('random.randint', side_effect=[4]):
...         play_turn("Player 2")
Player 2 rolled a 4
Player 2's turn total is 4
4
"""
```

I accepted the changes and saved the file. Then, I ran the tests again. This time, one of the tests in play_turn() passed, but the other test in play_turn() failed with the following info.

Failure info for the play_turn test

```
*****************************************************************************
File "c:\murach\ai\ch3\pig\pigdice.py", line 37, in __main__.play_turn
Failed example:
    with patch('builtins.input', side_effect=['y', 'n']):
        with patch('random.randint', side_effect=[5, 6, 1]):
            play_turn("Player 1")
Expected:
    Player 1 rolled a 5
    Player 1 rolled a 6
    Player 1 rolled a 1
    Player 1's turn total is 0
    0
Got:
    Player 1 rolled a 5
    Player 1 rolled a 6
    Player 1's turn total is 11
    11
```

To figure out why the test failed, I needed to better understand the doctest code that Copilot generated. To do that, I switched to the code editor, selected the code that uses patch(), right-clicked it, and selected Copilot ▶ Explain. When I did, Copilot generated the explanation shown next.

Copilot explanation of the doctest

The provided code snippet is a unit test for the `play_turn` function, which is part of a Pig dice game implementation. This test uses the `unittest.mock` module to simulate user input and dice rolls, ensuring that the function behaves as expected under controlled conditions. By using mocks, the test can provide specific inputs and observe the function's outputs without relying on actual user interaction or random number generation.

First, the `patch` function from the `unittest.mock` module is imported. The `patch` function allows you to temporarily replace the target object with a mock object during the test. This is useful for isolating the function being tested from external dependencies, such as user input or random number generation, which can introduce variability and make tests less predictable.

In the first `patch` context, the `input` function from the `builtins` module is replaced with a mock that returns predefined values. The `side_effect` parameter is set to `['y', 'n']`, meaning that the first call to `input` will return 'y' (indicating the user wants to roll again), and the second call will return 'n' (indicating the user wants to stop). This simulates a user who first chooses to continue playing and then decides to stop after the second roll.

In the second `patch` context, the `random.randint` function is replaced with a mock that returns predefined values. The `side_effect` parameter is set to `[5, 6, 1]`, meaning that the first call to `random.randint` will return 5, the second call will return 6, and the third call will return 1. This simulates the rolling of dice with specific outcomes. Within these patched contexts, the `play_turn` function is called with the argument `"Player 1"`. This setup allows the test to verify how `play_turn` handles the specific sequence of user inputs and dice rolls, ensuring that the function's behavior is consistent and correct under these conditions.

I read through this explanation, and it helped me understand what's going wrong with the doctest code. When the test executes, the player rolls a 5 and responds 'y' when prompted to roll again. Then, the player rolls a 6 and responds 'n' when prompted to roll again. Since the player responded 'n', the third roll that the test expects doesn't happen. Instead, the function displays the total points for the turn and returns those points, as you can see in the Got section of the test results.

To get this test to produce the results that the test expects, the side_effect variable for the input() function should contain 'y' and 'y', not 'y' and 'n'. That way, the third roll happens. I could ask Copilot to make this change, but I decided that it would be faster to change it myself. So, I manually changed the side_effect variable, saved the change, and ran the tests again. This time, all of the tests passed.

Improve the initial code

So far, I've used Copilot to create a Pig dice game that works and has some doctests that pass. At this point, I decided I wanted to improve the user interface.

Add a graphical representation of a die

First, I wanted the program to display a graphical representation of a die. For example, if the user rolls a 5, I want the program to display the following graphical representation.

A graphical representation for a die roll of 5

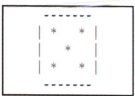

To do this, I decided to create a print_die() function that accepts a die number and prints a graphical representation of the die to the Terminal. I created this function by typing in the code editor, rather than using the Chat window. That's because I wanted to include doctests to show Copilot how the output should display.

To start, I typed the function signature, and pressed Enter. When I did, Copilot displayed the following suggestion in italics.

The print_die() function signature with suggested code

```
def print_die(roll):
    """

    Print an ASCII representation of a six-sided die with
```

I pressed Tab to accept the suggestion, and pressed Enter to get more suggestions. Copilot made an args suggestion, which I accepted. Copilot's next suggestion was to end the comments. However, I wanted to include doctests. So, I manually typed a doctests label and pressed Enter. In response, Copilot generated some doctests, which I accepted. I continued to press Enter to generate code and Tab to accept it until Copilot had generated the following comments, doctests, and code.

The print_die() function

```python
def print_die(roll):
    """
    Print an ASCII representation of a six-sided die with
    the given roll.

    Args:
        roll (int): The number rolled on the die.

    Doctest:
    >>> print_die(1)
     -------
    |       |
    |   *   |
    |       |
     -------
    >>> print_die(2)
     -------
    | *     |
    |       |
    |     * |
     -------
    """
    die = [
        "  ------- ",
        "|       |",
        "|   *   |",
        "|       |",
        "  ------- "
    ]
    if roll == 1:
        die[2] = "|       |"
    elif roll == 2:
        die[1] = "| *     |"
        die[3] = "|     * |"
    elif roll == 3:
        die[1] = "| *     |"
        die[2] = "|   *   |"
        die[3] = "|     * |"
    elif roll == 4:
        die[1] = "| *   * |"
        die[3] = "| *   * |"
    elif roll == 5:
        die[1] = "| *   * |"
        die[2] = "|   *   |"
        die[3] = "| *   * |"
    elif roll == 6:
        die[1] = "| * * * |"
        die[3] = "| * * * |"
    for line in die:
        print(line)
```

After reading this code, I wondered if it would display the dice correctly. Since the basic die starts with a dot in the middle of the second line, it seems like that might mess up the display for 2, 4, and 6, which shouldn't have any dots in the middle. In addition, it looks like the if statement for 1 removes the middle dot.

When I ran the tests, both tests failed, as expected, as shown next.

Test results for die value of 1

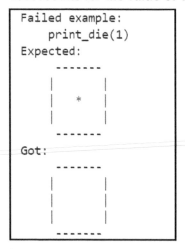

```
Failed example:
    print_die(1)
Expected:
    -------
    |     |
    |  *  |
    |     |
    -------
Got:
    -------
    |     |
    |     |
    |     |
    -------
```

Test results for die value of 2

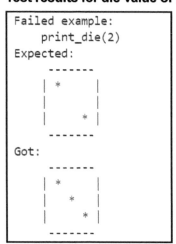

```
Failed example:
    print_die(2)
Expected:
    -------
    | *   |
    |     |
    |   * |
    -------
Got:
    -------
    | *   |
    |  *  |
    |   * |
    -------
```

I could have asked Copilot to adjust the code, but it was a simple fix, so I did it myself. To start, I removed the dot from the middle of the base die. Then, I added it to the if statement for 1. When I was done, I ran the tests again and, unexpectedly, they still failed.

Test results for die value 1

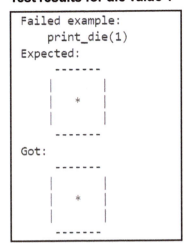

```
Failed example:
    print_die(1)
Expected:
    -------
    |     |
    |  *  |
    |     |
    -------
Got:
    -------
    |     |
    |  *  |
    |     |
    -------
```

Test results for die value 2

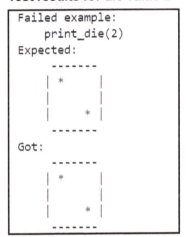

```
Failed example:
    print_die(2)
Expected:
    -------
    | *   |
    |     |
    |   * |
    -------
Got:
    -------
    | *   |
    |     |
    |   * |
    -------
```

I suspected that this problem was probably due to extra spaces or missing spaces in the expected results of the doctests. To find a fix, I switched to the Chat window and entered the following prompt.

A prompt for fixing the failing tests

> The doctests for print_die() are failing. Is there an extra space somewhere? Can you fix this issue?

In the past, I've had good results with asking Copilot to clean up extra or missing spaces. This time, however, Copilot couldn't do it. I tried three different prompts, and each time it made zero changes. Ultimately, I had to fix this problem myself, by making sure the spaces in the expected results of the doctests matched the spaces in the print statements of the code.

After I made and saved my changes, I ran the tests again, and they all passed. So, I used the following prompt to ask Copilot to use the new function.

A prompt in the Chat window to use the print_die() function

In response, Copilot suggested updates to the code and to the doctests. I accepted the suggestions and saved the file. Then, I ran the tests to make sure they still passed, and they did.

After running the tests, I ran the main() function to play the game. When I did, I was able to play the game in the Terminal as shown next.

The updated game in the Terminal

```
Let's Play Pig!
Pig Dice Game Rules:
1. The game is played by two players: Player 1 and Player 2.
2. Players take turns to roll a die as many times as they wish, adding the rolled
value to a turn total.
3. If a player rolls a 1, they score nothing for that turn and it becomes the next
player's turn.
4. A player can choose to hold (stop rolling) to add their turn total to their score.
5. The first player to reach or exceed 20 points wins the game.
Player 1 rolled a 4
-------
| *   * |
|       |
| *   * |
-------
Player 1, do you want to roll again? (y/n) y
Player 1 rolled a 4
-------
| *   * |
|       |
| *   * |
-------
Player 1, do you want to roll again? (y/n) n
Player 1's turn total is 8
Player 1's score: 8
Player 2's score: 0
Player 2 rolled a 5
-------
| *   * |
|   *   |
| *   * |
-------
Player 2, do you want to roll again? (y/n)
```

Better! But, the user interface still has a lot of duplicated text, which makes it hard to read.

Format the player scores

To make the user interface more readable, I decided to add some formatting to the player's scores. Once again, I decided to type the function into the code editor so I could use the doctest to specify the formatting for the scoreboard.

To start, I typed the signature for a function named print_scoreboard(). Then, I typed the following docstring comment and a doctest.

The signature and doctest for print_scoreboard()

```
def print_scoreboard(player1_score, player2_score):
    """
    Print the current scores of Player 1 and Player 2.

    Args:
        player1_score (int): The score of Player 1.
        player2_score (int): The score of Player 2.

    >>> print_scoreboard(10, 15)
    ****************
    *  SCOREBOARD   *
    ****************
    Player 1: 10
    Player 2: 15
    ****************
    """
```

As I typed, Copilot made suggestions for the description and arguments part of the comment, and I accepted those suggestions by pressing Tab. But, none of the suggestions for the doctest were what I wanted the output to look like, so I typed this output myself.

When I was done with the comment, I pressed Enter and Copilot suggested the following code. Then, I pressed Tab to accept that suggestion.

The generated code for print_scoreboard()

```
print("****************")
print("*  SCOREBOARD   *")
print("****************")
print(f"Player 1: {player1_score}")
print(f"Player 2: {player2_score}")
print("****************")
```

At this point, I saved the file and ran the tests. All of them passed.

Since the print_scoreboard() function passed its test, I asked Copilot to update the play_game() function to use it. Then, I accepted the changes that Copilot suggested, saved the file, and ran the tests. All of the tests passed, so I ran the game as shown next.

The game with the updated scoreboard

```
Player 1 rolled a 2
 -------
| *     |
|       |
|     * |
 -------
Player 1, do you want to roll again? (y/n) n
Player 1's turn total is 2
****************
*  SCOREBOARD  *
****************
Player 1: 2
Player 2: 7
****************
Player 2 rolled a 2
 -------
| *     |
|       |
|     * |
 -------
Player 2, do you want to roll again? (y/n)
```

Nice! But I thought that some blank lines above and below the scoreboard would improve the appearance of the user interface.

A prompt to add whitespace

Please update the print_scoreboard() function to add a blank line before and after the scoreboard.

At this point, Copilot suggested changes to the code and the doctests of the print_scoreboard() function. I accepted the changes, saved the file, and ran the tests. When I did, the test for the print_scoreboard() function failed with the following info.

The failure info for the test

```
Failed example:
    print_scoreboard(10, 15)
Expected nothing
Got:
    <BLANKLINE>
    ****************
    *  SCOREBOARD  *
    ****************
    Player 1: 10
    Player 2: 15
    ****************
    <BLANKLINE>
```

After studying this info and the updated doctest, I realized that Copilot added blank lines to the expected results of the doctest, like this:

The doctest that fails

```
>>> print_scoreboard(10, 15)

****************
*  SCOREBOARD  *
****************
Player 1: 10
Player 2: 15
****************

"""
```

However, the doctest interprets that initial blank line to mean that there are no expected results.

To fix this, the expected results need to include the <BLANKLINE> value that displays in the Got section of the test results. To me, it seemed easier to type this value into the code editor myself rather than ask Copilot to do it. So, that's what I did. But either approach would work.

The updated doctest

```
>>> print_scoreboard(10, 15)
<BLANKLINE>
****************
*  SCOREBOARD  *
****************
Player 1: 10
Player 2: 15
****************
<BLANKLINE>
"""
```

After fixing the doctest, I saved the file and ran the tests. This time, all of the tests passed. Then, I ran the game as shown next.

The game with the blank lines

```
Player 1 rolled a 4
 -------
| *   * |
|       |
| *   * |
 -------
Player 1, do you want to roll again? (y/n) n
Player 1's turn total is 4

****************
*  SCOREBOARD  *
****************
Player 1: 9
Player 2: 5
****************

Player 2 rolled a 3
```

```
--------
| *    |
|   *  |
|    * |
--------
Player 2, do you want to roll again? (y/n)
```

I though this looked pretty good, but I still wanted to improve the way the program displays each turn.

Format the player turn

Instead of printing "Player {} rolled a {}", I'd like the program to print "PLAYER {}'s TURN" at the start of the turn. After that, I'd like the program to only print the die.

I decided to make this change in the code editor. Specifically, I decided to change the expected results of the doctests and let Copilot use the doctests as a guide to generate the new code.

To do that, first I deleted the existing code in the player_turn() function. Then, I modified the doctests so they looked the way I wanted, pressed Enter to generate the new code, and pressed Tab to accept it. This resulted in the following code.

The updated doctest and code

```
>>> from unittest.mock import patch
>>> with patch('builtins.input', side_effect=['y', 'y']):
...     with patch('random.randint', side_effect=[5, 6, 1]):
...         play_turn("Player 1")
PLAYER 1's TURN

-------
| *   * |
|   *   |
| *   * |

-------

-------
| * * * |
|       |
| * * * |

-------

-------
|       |
|   *   |
|       |

-------
Player 1's turn total is 0
0
>>> with patch('builtins.input', side_effect=['n']):
...     with patch('random.randint', side_effect=[4]):
...         play_turn("Player 2")
PLAYER 2's TURN

-------
| *   * |
|       |
| *   * |

-------
```

```
    Player 2's turn total is 4
    4
    """
    print(f"{player}'s TURN")
    turn_total = 0
    roll = roll_die()
    while roll != 1:
        print_die(roll)
        turn_total += roll
        print(f"{player}'s turn total is {turn_total}")
        choice = input("Roll again? (y/n) ")
        if choice.lower() == 'n':
            return turn_total
        roll = roll_die()
    print_die(roll)
    print(f"{player} rolled a 1! No points earned this turn.")
    return 0
```

This new code moves the player's turn total after each roll of the die. I didn't ask for that, but it was something I wanted to do later anyway. However, it looked to me like this change would make the first doctest fail, so I ran the tests again.

Interestingly, both doctests failed. The second failed because the expected results didn't include the turn total. And, both tests failed because they expect the initial "PLAYER {}'s TURN" to be capitalized. I switched to the Chat window and entered the following prompt.

A prompt for fixing the player_turn() function

Please update player_turn() to print the player's turn in all caps and print "Total is n" after each roll of the die. Make sure the doctests are updated to have correct expected output.

I accepted the changes Copilot generated, saved the file and ran the tests. This time, all of the tests passed. So, I ran the game and tested the new user interface.

The game with formatted player's turn

```
PLAYER 1's TURN
-------
| * * * |
|       |
| * * * |
-------
Total is 6
Roll again? (y/n) y
-------
| *   * |
|   *   |
| *   * |
-------
Total is 11
Roll again? (y/n) n
Player 1's turn total is 11
```

```
****************
*  SCOREBOARD   *
****************
Player 1: 11
Player 2: 0
****************

PLAYER 2's TURN
 -------
|  *    |
|       |
|    *  |
 -------
Total is 2
Roll again? (y/n)
```

Looks good! However, I decided that I didn't want to display the "Player X's turn total is X" line. I also decided to add blank lines before and after the rules and to adjust the location of the "Let's play Pig!" message.

To do that, I used the following prompts. I divided these tasks into separate prompts because I didn't want to ask Copilot to do too much at once.

The first prompt

> Please remove the "Player ... turn total is…" line from the play_turn() function.

The second prompt

> Please add a line before and after displaying the rules. Use the ~ character for the line.

The third prompt

> Please move the "Let's play Pig!" message after the rules. Also, please add a blank line before and after "Let's play Pig!" Use the \n character to add each blank line.

After each prompt, I accepted the proposed changes. When all the changes were accepted, I save the file and ran the tests, which all passed. Then, I ran the game in the Terminal as shown next.

The updated game in the Terminal

```
~~~~~~~~~~~~~~~~~~~~~~~~~~~~~~~~~~~~~~~~~~~~~~~~~~~~~~~~~~
Pig Dice Game Rules:
1. The game is played by two players: Player 1 and Player 2.
2. Players take turns to roll a die as many times as they wish, adding the rolled
value to a turn total.
3. If a player rolls a 1, they score nothing for that turn and it becomes the next
player's turn.
4. A player can choose to hold (stop rolling) to add their turn total to their score.
5. The first player to reach or exceed 20 points wins the game.
~~~~~~~~~~~~~~~~~~~~~~~~~~~~~~~~~~~~~~~~~~~~~~~~~~~~~~~~~~

Let's Play Pig!

PLAYER 1's TURN
 - - - - - - -
|         |
|    *    |
|         |
 - - - - - - -
Player 1 rolled a 1! No points earned this turn.

****************
*  SCOREBOARD   *
****************
Player 1: 0
Player 2: 0
****************

PLAYER 2's TURN
 - - - - - - -
|  *    *  |
|    *    |
|  *    *  |
 - - - - - - -
Total is 5
Roll again? (y/n)
```

Nice! The game works as expected and the user interface is easy to use and read.

Refactor the code

Once you've got your code working the way you want, it's a good practice to review the code and see if there's anything that can be improved. This is called *refactoring* your code, and Copilot can help with that too.

Ask Copilot for advice

When I reviewed the code for the Pig dice game, I thought it might work better if it used an object rather than functions. That way, it would be easier to make future changes like allowing the user to enter their name or set the winning point total. I switched to the Chat window and asked Copilot what it thought.

The prompt in the Chat window

> Would it be better to use an object rather than functions?

When I did, Copilot gave me the following response, along with suggested code for a class named PigDice.

Copilot's response (part 1)

> 🐙 GitHub Copilot
>
> › Used 2 references
>
> Yes, using an object-oriented approach can make the code more modular, easier to maintain, and extend. Here is a refactored version of your code using classes:

Copilot's response (part 2)

> This refactoring encapsulates the game logic within a `PigGame` class, making it easier to manage the state and behavior of the game.

Convert from functions to objects

Copilot's responses convinced me that using the PigGame class was a good idea. At this point, I wanted to accept the PigGame class that Copilot suggested. However, I didn't want to overwrite my existing code, so I decided to save the proposed code in a new file. To do that, I used the following prompt.

A prompt to write the code in a new file

> Can you write the code for the PigGame class to a new file named pigdice_object.py?

Copilot didn't actually create a new file in response to this prompt. Instead, it generated proposed code in the Chat window for a new file named pigdice_object.py. To write this code to the new file, I clicked the Apply icon as shown next.

The Apply icon for the new file

```
import random                                    ⟳  ⑧  ▯  ⋯
import doctest                          ┌─────────────────────────┐
                                        │ Apply to pigdice_object.py │
                                        └─────────────────────────┘
class PigGame:
```

Since that Python file didn't exist yet, VS Code used the following dialog to ask me how I wanted to proceed.

The dialog to write the changes

```
┌────────────────────────────────────────────────────────────┐
│ Select where to apply the code block                         │
├────────────────────────────────────────────────────────────┤
│ New file 'pigdice_object.py'                                 │
│ New untitled editor                                          │
│ Active editor 'pigdice.py'                                   │
└────────────────────────────────────────────────────────────┘
```

To write the code to the new file, I selected "New file". Then, Copilot created the pigdice_object.py file and wrote the code to it. Some of the code for the PigGame class that Copilot wrote to the new file is shown next. Note that this code includes updated doctests.

Some of the code for the PigGame class

```python
import random
import doctest

class PigGame:
    def __init__(self):
        self.scores = {"Player 1": 0, "Player 2": 0}
        self.winning_total = 20

    def roll_die(self):
        """
        Roll a six-sided die and return the result.

        >>> result = PigGame().roll_die()
        >>> 1 <= result <= 6
        True
        """
        return random.randint(1, 6)

    def play_turn(self, player):
        """
        Play a single turn for the given player.

        Args:
            player (str): The name of the player ("Player 1" or "Player 2").

        Returns:
            int: The total points scored by the player in this turn.
```

```
Doctest:
>>> from unittest.mock import patch
>>> with patch('builtins.input', side_effect=['y', 'y']):
...     with patch('random.randint', side_effect=[5, 6, 1]):
...         PigGame().play_turn("Player 1")
PLAYER 1'S TURN
 -------
| *   * |
|   *   |
| *   * |
 -------
Total is 5
 -------
| * * * |
|       |
| * * * |
 -------
Total is 11
 -------
|       |
|   *   |
|       |
 -------
Player 1 rolled a 1! No points earned this turn.
0
>>> with patch('builtins.input', side_effect=['n']):
...     with patch('random.randint', side_effect=[4]):
...         PigGame().play_turn("Player 2")
PLAYER 2'S TURN
 -------
| *   * |
|       |
| *   * |
 -------
Total is 4
4
"""
print(f"{player.upper()}'S TURN")
turn_total = 0
roll = self.roll_die()
while roll != 1:
    self.print_die(roll)
    turn_total += roll
    print(f"Total is {turn_total}")
    choice = input("Roll again? (y/n) ")
    if choice.lower() == 'n':
        return turn_total
    roll = self.roll_die()
self.print_die(roll)
print(f"{player} rolled a 1! No points earned this turn.")
return 0

def play_game(self):
    """
    Play a game of Pig between Player 1 and Player 2.
    Returns:
        bool: True if the game should be played again,
        False otherwise.
    """
```

```
        self.scores = {"Player 1": 0, "Player 2": 0}
        while (self.scores["Player 1"] < self.winning_total and
                self.scores["Player 2"] < self.winning_total):
            for player in ["Player 1", "Player 2"]:
                self.scores[player] += self.play_turn(player)
                self.print_scoreboard()
                if self.scores[player] >= self.winning_total:
                    print(f"{player} wins!")
                    again = input("Do you want to play again? (y/n) ").lower()
                    return again == 'y'
        return False

if __name__ == "__main__":
    doctest.testmod(verbose=True)
```

Run the program

After creating the new file, I saved it and ran the tests. They all passed. At this point, I still needed to change the main() function to use the new PigGame class. To do that, I switched to the Chat window in Edit mode and entered the following prompt.

The prompt to update the main() function

Update the main() function to use the PigGame object from pigdice_object.py.

The updated code that uses the PigGame class

```
from pigdice_object import PigGame

def main():
    game = PigGame()
    game.display_rules()
    print("\nLet's play Pig!\n")
    while game.play_game():
        pass
    print("Thanks for playing!")

if __name__ == "__main__":
    main()
```

I accepted the changes and saved the file. Then, I ran the game, and it worked the same as before.

Perspective

Although the Pig program presented in this chapter isn't as long and complex as most real-world software, it begins to show how helpful Copilot can be when developing software.

First, this chapter shows how to switch between various features of Copilot. That includes the Chat window, the autocomplete feature, and the explain command. In addition, it shows some cases where it makes sense to manually edit the code.

Second, this chapter shows how to use doctests as part of the development process. Specifically, it shows how to use doctests to provide context that Copilot can use to generate code and to quickly test the code that's generated by Copilot. This is important since Copilot often generates code that doesn't work correctly.

Third, this chapter shows how you can use Copilot to convert a function-based program to an object-oriented program. This is often helpful when developing longer programs.

Terms

doctest

refactoring

Exercises

1. Create a Python program that works like the Pig program presented in this chapter.
2. Create a Python program that that lets you play a game of Blackjack against a dealer.
3. Convert the command-line interface (CLI) for the Pig program presented in this chapter to a graphical user interface (GUI).
4. Refactor the Pig program presented in this chapter so it uses a class named Die to encapsulate the functionality for a die object.
5. Enhance the Pig program presented in this chapter so it allows players to enter their names and specify a winning point total.

Chapter 4

Create a website

This chapter shows how you can use Copilot to create a website. To do that, it shows how I used Copilot to start a website for an organization named San Joaquin Valley Town Hall that hosts a lecture series with different guest speakers every month. Due to the nondeterministic nature of LLMs, the prompts shown in this chapter won't work the same for you as they did for me. However, they illustrate a thought process that you can use when working with Copilot. In addition, the prompts show how to handle many of the typical issues that arise when using Copilot to create a website.

Start the website **100**
Examine the starting files 100
Create a directory structure 101
Develop the home page 103
Develop a speaker page.. 106

Refine the web pages **107**
Fix the content for the home page.. 107
Refine the shared code 108
Refine the header.. 109

Fix two responsive design issues...**111**
Scale the images.. 111
Add a menu toggle for small screens.. 113

Refactor the website **117**
Use nested styles 118
Add a submenu to the navbar... 120
Add comments to HTML and CSS files... 125

Perspective..**126**

Start the website

To start the Town Hall website, I decided to create initial versions of the two pages for which I already had text and images. To create these pages, I needed to create the directories and files that they needed, and I needed to modify the HTML and CSS for those pages until I was satisfied with their initial versions.

Examine the starting files

Before getting started, I examined the starting files for this website that were provided to me. This included the following image files.

The files in the images folder

File	Description
favicon.ico	The favicon for the website.
logo.gif	The Town Hall logo.
sampson.jpg	A picture of the speaker named Scott Sampson.

In addition, the starting files included two text files that contained the text for two pages of the website. For example, the following index.txt file contains the text for the home page.

The index.txt file that contains the text for the home page

```
San Joaquin Valley Town Hall
Bringing cutting-edge speakers to the valley

Home | Speakers | Get Tickets | Become a Member | About Us

This season's guest speakers

October: David Brancaccio
November: Andrew Ross Sorkin
January: Amy Chua
February: Scott Sampson
March: Carlos Eire
April: Ronan Tynan

Looking for a unique gift?

For only $100, you can get a book of tickets for all of the remaining speakers, plus
a second book of tickets for a companion.

Or, for $50, you can give yourself the gift of our speakers, and still get an extra
ticket for a companion, but for just one of the events.

Contact us by phone at (559) 555-1212 for ticket information.

Lecture notes
Event change for November
```

```
Ross Sorkin. The appearance of previously scheduled speaker, Greg Mortenson, has
been postponed.

Lecture day, time, and location
All one-hour lectures are on the second Wednesday of the month beginning at 10:30 a.m.
at William Saroyan Theatre, 700 M Street, Fresno, CA.

Copyright San Joaquin Valley Town Hall.
```

The starting files also included a text file named sampson.txt that contains the text for a web page for an upcoming speaker named Scott Sampson.

Create a directory structure

To create the directory structure for the website, I opened the Chat window. By default, it was in Ask mode, which is what I wanted. So, I entered the following prompt.

A prompt to start the Town Hall website

> I need to create a website called Town Hall that presents a series of lectures with guest speakers. Here are some specifications for the site:
>
> * Use HTML and CSS.
> * Don't use JavaScript.
> * Store the images in a folder named images.
> * Provide an .html file for the home page and a speaker named sampson.
>
> Can you suggest a structure for this website and help me create it?

This prompt provided some general information about the website, some specifications for what languages to use, and some specifications for the directories and files for the website. When I entered this prompt, Copilot proposed the following directory structure.

The proposed directory structure

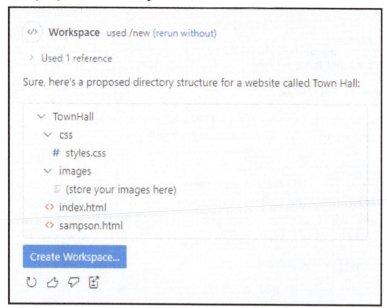

I reviewed this proposed structure and decided that it was good enough to use as a starting point, so I clicked the Create Workspace button. This created the initial directories and files for my site.

After Copilot created the structure for the website, I copied the image files into the images folder, and I copied the text files into the root folder. In addition, I used VS Code's Explorer window to rename the root folder for the website to town-hall. When I was done, I had the following directory structure and starting files.

The edited directory structure with the starting files

Since this directory structure is simple, having Copilot create it didn't save me a lot of time. However, Copilot is capable of creating much more complex directory structures, which can save a lot of time.

After making sure the starting files were in place, I examined the code in the HTML files and the CSS file and found that they already contained HTML and CSS that provided a starting point for the website. However, the HTML files didn't contain the correct content for the pages yet.

Develop the home page

At this point, I decided to work on the index.html file to get it to display the correct content for the home page. To do that, I opened the index.html and index.txt files in the code editor. Then, I switched the Chat window to Edit mode, made sure the HTML, CSS, and TXT files were attached, and entered the following prompt.

Modify the index.html and styles.css file according to the following specifications:

* The attached index.txt file contains the text for the index.html page.
* The home page should have a top navbar with links for Home, Speakers, Get Tickets, Become a Member, and About Us.
* Use flexbox layout.
* Use a responsive web design.
* Use a two-column layout for wide screens.
* Use a single-column layout for narrow screens.

After entering this prompt, Copilot suggested changes, and they looked good to me, so I accepted them. Then, I tested the home page by running it in a browser on a large screen as shown next.

The home page displayed on a large screen

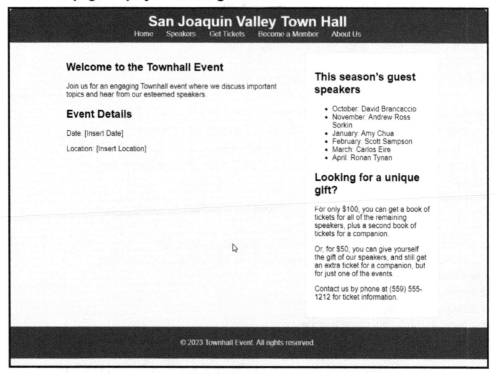

When I reviewed this page, I could see that Copilot had successfully added a *navigation menu*, also known as a *navbar*, to the top of the screen.

However, I could also see that Copilot made several mistakes. First, it added text that wasn't in the index.txt file to the main content and pushed the content that should be in the main section into the sidebar. Second, it didn't include some of the provided content, such as the lecture information. Third, the footer was different than the provided text. And fourth, Copilot left out the page subtitle. This shows that it's important to carefully compare the expected content with the actual content. At this point, I decided to leave this incorrect content and continue testing the responsive design by narrowing the width of the browser as shown next.

The home page on a small screen

This shows that the page switches from a two-column format on large screens to a one-column format on smaller screens, which is what I wanted. So, although I still needed to fix the content for this page, I thought the page layout looked good enough to continue on by developing an initial version of the speaker page.

Develop a speaker page

With an initial version of the home page working, I prompted Copilot to generate the content for the speaker page. To do that, I used the following prompt. In the interest of brevity, this chapter doesn't show the content of the sampson.txt file, but I attached this file before I entered the following prompt.

A prompt for creating the sampson.html page

> Modify the sampson.html file according to these specifications:
>
> * The attached sampson.txt file contains the text for the sampson.html page.
> * The sampson.html file should use a similar format to the index.html file.

When I entered this prompt, Copilot suggested some changes, and I accepted them. Then, I opened the sampson.html file in a web browser as shown next.

The sampson.html page in a web browser

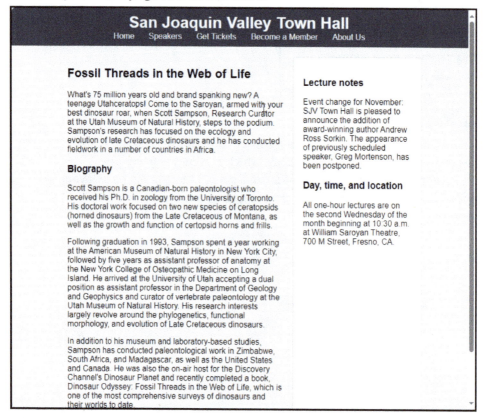

This time, Copilot successfully transferred the content of the text file into the HTML file. However, there were still some minor issues. For example, this page used the same incorrect footer as the home page. Regardless, I was satisfied with the initial version of this page, so I moved back to the home page to refine it.

Refine the web pages

After creating the initial pages, I needed to refine the pages. In particular, I decided to fix the following issues.

Issues to fix

- Fix the content for the home page.
- Add images to both pages.
- Fix the links in the navbar so they work.
- Improve the appearance of the navbar.

Fix the content for the home page

To start, I decided to fix the content for the home page. To do that, I copied the missing content from the index.txt file into the prompt in the Chat window and entered some additional text to create the following prompt. In this case, I decided to provide the content for the aside as text within the prompt because I wanted to make sure that Copilot wouldn't get confused.

A prompt for fixing the content issues in the index.html file

> Please fix the following issues with the index.html file:
> * Delete the existing content in the main section.
> * Move the existing content in the aside to the main section.
> * Add the following content to the aside.
>
> Lecture notes
> Event change for November: SJV Town Hall is pleased to announce the addition of award-winning author Andrew Ross Sorkin. The appearance of previously scheduled speaker, Greg Mortenson, has been postponed.
>
> Day, time, and location
> All one-hour lectures are on the second Wednesday of the month beginning at 10:30 a.m. at William Saroyan Theatre, 700 M Street, Fresno, CA.

After I entered this prompt, Copilot suggested changes that fixed this issue, so I accepted them.

Note that the previous prompt only addresses issues that are specific to the home page. It doesn't address any issues that are shared between the home page and the speaker page such as the wrong content in the footer. That's because you should make all changes to shared elements at the same time so that it's easier to make sure the shared elements match for all pages.

Refine the shared code

After fixing the content on the home page, I decided to fix the minor issues that are common to both pages. To do that, I entered the following prompt.

A prompt for fixing shared issues

Modify the sampson.html and the index.html files.
* Use the images/favicon.ico file as the favicon.
* Display the images/logo.gif file at the top.
* Remove 2023 from the footer.

When I entered this prompt and accepted the suggested changes, Copilot fixed the favicon and footer issues and displayed the image at the top of the header as shown next.

The logo at the top of the header

To finish adding images to the web pages, I decided to add the sampson.jpg image to the sampson.html page. To do that, I entered the following prompt.

A prompt for adding the sampson.jpg file to the sampson.html file

Add the sampson.jpg image under the <h2> tag in the content section of the sampson.html file.

When I accepted the suggested changes, Copilot added the image as shown next.

The image on the sampson.html page

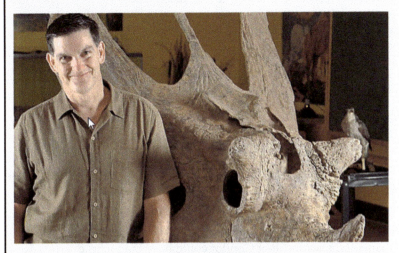

Fossil Threads in the Web of Life

What's 75 million years old and brand spanking new? A teenage Utahceratops! Come to the Saroyan, armed with your best dinosaur roar, when Scott Sampson, Research Curator at the Utah Museum of Natural History, steps to the podium. Sampson's research has focused on the ecology and evolution of late Cretaceous dinosaurs and he has conducted fieldwork in a number of countries in Africa.

Biography

Lecture notes

Event change for November: SJV Town Hall is pleased to announce the addition of award-winning author Andrew Ross Sorkin. The appearance of previously scheduled speaker, Greg Mortenson, has been postponed.

Day, time, and location

All one-hour lectures are on the second Wednesday of the month beginning at

Refine the header

At this point, I thought the content for the pages looked good, but I thought I could improve the appearance of the header, which is shown next.

The header

To improve the appearance of this header, I entered the following prompt to address several issues with the navbar.

A prompt to address the navbar issues

Please make the following changes to the nav element:
* Add some margin between the nav and the h1 element above it.
* Increase the font size of the navbar links.
* Increase the top margin between the navbar and the page title.
* Add a visual indication of which link is currently active.

After I accepted the suggested changes, I opened the home page in a browser, and I thought the styling of the navbar looked much better.

However, I still wanted to adjust the colors of the header and footer to match the color of the logo. Since Copilot is text-based, it can't analyze the logo to determine its color. As a result, I determined the RGB color of the logo by using an online RGB color picker and matching it to orange color of the logo. This color picker indicated that the hex value for this color is #f2972e.

It seemed easy enough to set the header and footer to this color and the background color of the <nav> element to black. So, I opened the CSS file and made these changes manually. I suspect that Copilot could have made these changes for me, if I had entered a prompt and supplied it with the hex value for the orange color, but it seemed easier to make this change myself. After changing the CSS file, I opened the home page in a browser as shown next.

The home page after the navbar and color changes

Fix two responsive design issues

After the color changes, I was satisfied with how the website looked on large screens. However, when I tested it on small screens, I found two issues that I wanted to fix.

Scale the images

When I opened the sampson.html in a browser and made the screen width narrow, the browser cut of the right side of the image and the text above and below it.

An image that isn't scaling correctly

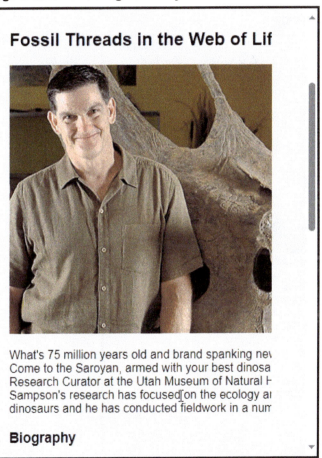

I reviewed the CSS for this page and determined that it didn't include any code to scale the image when the screen size changed. Then, I prompted Copilot to scale the image as shown next.

A prompt to scale the image

On the sampson.html page, the right side of the image and the text is getting cut off on small screens. Modify the styles.css file to make the image scale correctly.

Copilot's response suggested adding the following code to the CSS file.

The suggested CSS code

```css
img {
    max-width: 100%;
    height: auto;
}
```

After accepting the suggestion, I opened the web page in a browser and tested it on a smaller screen. It scaled correctly as shown next.

An image that scales correctly

Since the CSS code for fixing this issue applies to all <img> elements, it should also scale any other images that I add to the website later.

Add a menu toggle for small screens

When I displayed a web page on a small screen, the navbar was displayed vertically and used too much space at the top of the viewport as shown next.

The navigation menu on a small screen

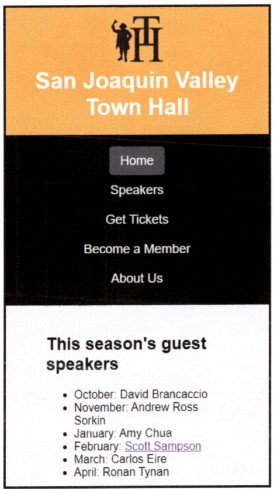

This is a bad design because it forces users to scroll down past the navigation menu to view the page content every time they navigate to a new page on a small screen. To fix this, you can have Copilot help you create a menu toggle for small screens. I attempted to do this by entering the following prompt.

A prompt for creating a responsive menu

For small screens, modify the CSS to implement a responsive navigation menu with these specifications:
* Use a checkbox toggle to open and close the menu.
* Display a hamburger icon when the menu is closed.
* Display an x icon when the menu is open.

The response from Copilot suggested adding some CSS that looked like it might work, so I accepted the suggestion. Then, I opened the home page in the browser.

On a large screen, the page didn't hide the checkbox for displaying the menu. Otherwise, the page worked as expected.

On a small screen, the page hid the navigation menu and displayed a hamburger menu icon as shown next.

A small screen with the hamburger menu icon

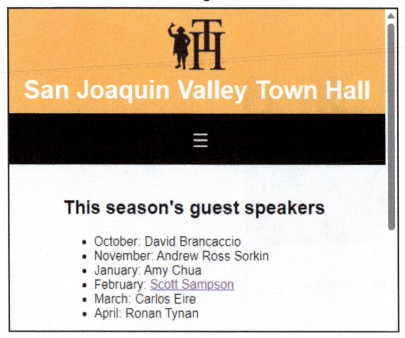

However, it displayed the hamburger menu icon in the middle of the page, and I wanted to display it on the left side of the page.

I continued testing by clicking on the hamburger menu icon. When I did that, the page displayed the navigation menu as shown next.

A small screen with the expanded navigation menu

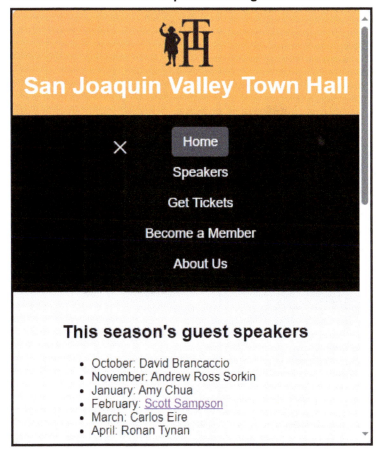

On the good side, the new CSS successfully displayed the menu and the close icon while also hiding the hamburger menu icon. On the bad side, it displayed the icon for closing the menu to the left of the menu rather than above it.

To fix the issues that I identified during testing, I entered the following prompt.

A prompt to address the issues for the responsive menu

> The CSS for the navbar still needs the following modifications:
> * Align the icons for the menu with the left side of the container.
> * On large screens, hide the checkbox.
> * On small screens, position the menu below the close icon.

When I did, Copilot suggested changes to the CSS that seemed like they might fix the problem, so I accepted them. Then, I viewed the pages in a browser again, and tested them on large and small screens, and it seemed to fix all of the issues. For example, on a small screen, the CSS hid the menu and displayed the hamburger menu icon as shown next.

A small screen when the menu is hidden

If I clicked on the hamburger menu icon, the CSS displayed the navigation menu as shown next.

A small screen when the menu is displayed

With this, I feel like navigation menu and both of the web pages are working fairly well!

Refactor the website

Now that two pages of the website are working well, you can *refactor* some of the code to make the website more readable or to improve existing features. Refactoring refers to the process of restructuring existing code to improve its structure or implementation.

Use nested styles

When I reviewed the CSS for this website, I noticed that it didn't use nested styles. Since nested styles can reduce code duplication and make the code easier to read, I decided to ask Copilot to refactor this code for me. To do this, I highlighted the following CSS because I wanted to refactor that code.

The CSS without nesting

```css
nav {
    justify-content: left;
    position: relative;
}

nav ul {
    display: none;
    flex-direction: column;
}

nav label {
    display: block;
    cursor: pointer;
    margin-left: 1em;
    font-size: 24px;
    color: white;
    background: black;
}

nav label::before {
    content: "\2630"; /* Hamburger icon */
}

nav input[type="checkbox"]:checked + label::before {
    content: "\2715"; /* X icon */
    justify-content: left;
}

nav input[type="checkbox"]:checked + label + ul {
    display: flex;
    position: absolute;
    top: 100%;
    left: 0;
    background-color: black;
    width: 100%;
    flex-direction: column;
}

nav ul li {
    margin: 10px 0;
}
```

Then, I pressed Ctrl+I to display the inline chat interface, and I entered the following prompt.

The prompt for nesting the CSS

Consolidate the selected code using CSS nesting.

When I entered this prompt, Copilot suggested the following code, and I accepted that suggestion. This removed many duplicate element names and used nested styles to clearly show the structure of the elements within the <nav> element.

The nested CSS

```css
nav {
    justify-content: left;
    position: relative;

    ul {
        display: none;
        flex-direction: column;

        li {
            margin: 10px 0;
        }
    }

    label {
        display: block;
        cursor: pointer;
        margin-left: 1em;
        font-size: 24px;
        color: white;
        background: black;

        &::before {
            content: "\2630"; /* Hamburger icon */
        }
    }

    input[type="checkbox"]:checked {
        + label::before {
            content: "\2715"; /* X icon */
            justify-content: left;
        }

        + label + ul {
            display: flex;
            position: absolute;
            top: 100%;
            left: 0;
            background-color: black;
            width: 100%;
            flex-direction: column;
        }
    }
}
```

If I wanted, I could have repeated this process for the rest of the rules in the CSS file. However, I decided that nesting the rules for the <nav> element was enough for now.

I also could have attempted to refactor the entire file in one shot. However, using a one-shot prompt can make it more difficult to check the modifications that Copilot is making. That's why I decided to break this task up into smaller tasks.

Add a submenu to the navbar

At this point, the Speakers link on the navbar navigated directly to the sampson.html page. This worked initially because there was only one speaker page, but the website needs to support multiple speakers. As a result, I wanted to modify the Speakers link to display a drop-down menu that allows the user to select one speaker from multiple speakers.

To implement this, I decided to start by modifying the HTML for both of the web pages. To do that, I attached both HTML files to the prompt in the Chat window. Then, I entered the following prompt.

A prompt to generate the HTML for the new Speakers item

Modify the attached HTML files to convert the Speakers link into a drop-down menu that allows the user to select either Sampson or Coming Soon. The Coming Soon link shouldn't have a target.

After I accepted the suggested code, the HTML for the <nav> element looked like this:

The HTML for a navbar with a submenu

```html
<nav class="navbar">
    <input type="checkbox" id="menu-toggle">
    <label for="menu-toggle"></label>
    <ul class="menu">
        <li><a href="index.html" class="active">Home</a></li>
        <li>
            <a href="#">Speakers</a>
            <ul class="submenu">
                <li><a href="sampson.html">Scott Sampson</a></li>
                <li><a href="#">Coming Soon</a></li>
            </ul>
        </li>
        <li><a href="tickets.html">Get Tickets</a></li>
        <li><a href="membership.html">Become a Member</a></li>
        <li><a href="about.html">About Us</a></li>
    </ul>
</nav>
```

Since this HTML looked good to me, I decided to modify the CSS to support the drop-down menu. To do that, I entered the following prompt.

The prompt for generating the CSS for the submenu

Given the HTML for the navbar, modify the CSS to display the Speakers submenu when the mouse hovers over the Speakers link.

After I entered this prompt, Copilot suggested the following CSS.

The CSS for the submenu

```css
nav ul.menu li {
    position: relative;
}

nav ul.menu li ul.submenu {
    display: none;
    position: absolute;
    top: 100%;
    left: 0;
    background-color: black;
    padding: 0;
    margin: 0;
    list-style: none;
    z-index: 1000;
}

nav ul.menu li:hover ul.submenu {
    display: block;
}

nav ul.menu li ul.submenu li {
    margin: 0;
}

nav ul.menu li ul.submenu li a {
    padding: 10px 15px;
    display: block;
    white-space: nowrap;
    color: white;
    text-decoration: none;
}

nav ul.menu li ul.submenu li a:hover {
    background-color: #575d63;
}
```

Since the suggested CSS didn't use nested styles to reduce code duplication and improve readability, I considered asking Copilot to nest these styles. However, I decided that I wanted to test the CSS first. So, I accepted this suggestion and opened the home page in a browser as shown next.

The submenu on a large screen

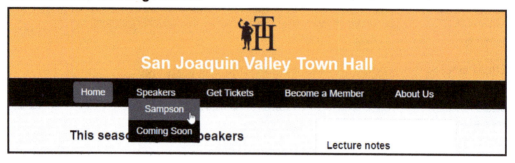

On this screen, there were still improvements that could be made. For example, I still wanted to display a down triangle to the right of the Speakers menu item to indicate that the Speakers item leads to a drop-down menu. However, I decided to test the web page on a small screen first. To do that, I narrowed the browser window as shown next.

The submenu on a small screen

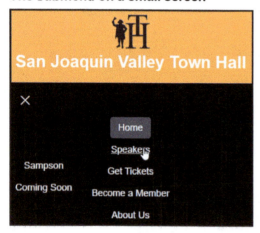

On a small screen, the submenu didn't work right for several reasons. First, the Speakers drop-down menu isn't aligned with the Speakers item that leads to it. Second, the drop-down menu doesn't have a border. Third, as on large screens, the Speakers item doesn't provide a visual indicator that it leads to a drop-down menu.

To address these issues, I decided to start with the two issues that apply to the way the submenu is displayed on small screens. To do that, I entered the following prompt. This prompt asks Copilot to modify the CSS for the submenu to display the submenu relative to the Speakers link, and it asks Copilot to add a border to the submenu.

The prompt for modifying the submenu

Modify the CSS for the submenu to:
* Display the submenu relative to its parent item.
* Add a 1px solid border that uses an appropriate light color.

The CSS with some code duplication

```css
nav ul.menu li ul.submenu {
    display: none;
    position: relative; /* Changed from absolute to relative */
    top: 100%;
    left: 0;
    background-color: black;
    border: #dddddd 1px solid;
    padding: 0;
    margin: 0;
    list-style: none;
    z-index: 1000;
}
```

Some of this code was unnecessary because it was already implemented earlier in the CSS file. To remove the code duplication, I selected the generated code and used the inline chat interface to enter the following prompt.

A prompt that removes code duplication

Remove any properties that are already set earlier in the CSS file.

When I accepted the changes, I was left with the following code.

The CSS with code duplication removed

```css
nav ul.menu li ul.submenu {
    position: relative; /* Changed from absolute to relative */
    border: #dddddd 1px solid;
}
```

At this point, I changed the code in both HTML files to include a down triangle as part of the Speakers link. To do that, I switched to the Chat window, added both files to the prompt, and entered the following prompt.

A prompt for adding a down triangle to the end of a link

Add a down triangle to the end of the Speakers link.

When I accepted the suggested changes and ran the web pages in a browser, the submenu displayed correctly on a small screen as shown next.

The submenu on a small screen

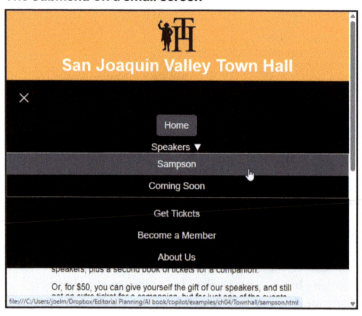

In addition, the submenu displayed correctly on a large screen as shown next.

The submenu on a large screen

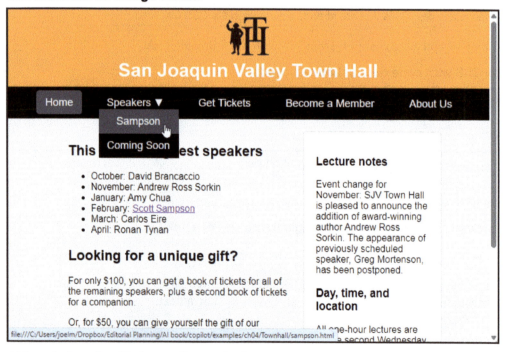

Although there is still plenty of room for improvement, I decided to stop the development of this website here for now.

Add comments to HTML and CSS files

Since the generated code didn't have any comments, I decided to further refactor this website by adding some comments to the HTML and CSS files. To do that, I entered the following prompt in the Chat window.

A prompt for adding comments to the HTML files

> Add comments that document the attached HTML files. Focus on describing what each section implements.

This prompt added comments to the main sections for each HTML file. However, Copilot skipped some sections in the sampson.html file. For example, it added comments for the sidebar and footer in the index.html file but didn't in the sampson.html file.

A prompt for adding comments to the CSS file

> Add comments to document the CSS rules in this file. Be sure to include the elements modified by nested styles.

This prompt added comments for each rule in the CSS file, including nested rules. This is a good start, but it's still good to go through each of these files and make sure that the comments accurately describe the code and that any code that's difficult to understand has comments.

Perspective

This chapter showed how to use Copilot to create the first two pages of a website. Then, it showed how to refactor and document the website. This website doesn't include any JavaScript that provides additional client-side functionality, and it doesn't use any other code to provide server-side processing. As a result, it's not as complex as most real-world websites. Still, the concepts and skills presented in this chapter provide a foundation for using Copilot to help you develop websites.

Terms

navigation menu

navbar

refactoring

Exercises

1. Improve the Town Hall website by displaying the Town Hall logo on the left side of the header, by adding "Bringing cutting-edge speakers to the valley" to the header, and by refactoring all of the CSS to use nested styles.

2. Add a page to the Town Hall website for a second speaker. This page should work like the sampson.html file, but it would have information about a different lecturer. Adjust the links and navigation menus to work correctly with this page.

3. Add a page to the Town Hall website for the Get Tickets link. This page should work like the index.html and sampson.html pages, but it should provide the information that's in the tickets.txt file that's in the town-hall-start folder.

4. Create a website about any subject that interests you. Ideally, pick a subject where you have some preexisting text and images that you can use. That way, you can focus on using Copilot to help you develop the code for the website.

Chapter 5

Work with a database

This chapter shows how to use Copilot to work with a database. In particular, it shows how to generate the SQL statements that you can use to work with a database.

To illustrate these skills, this chapter shows how to use a SQLite database. That's because you can use a SQLite database without needing to install a database server. By contrast, you need to install a database server to work with many other relational databases. But, since SQLite implements most of the SQL standards, the skills presented in this chapter also apply to other relational databases such as MySQL, SQL Server, and Oracle.

How to work with SQLite 128
Install DB Browser for SQLite 128
Open a database and view its tables 128
Run SQL statements 130
Export a schema... 131

Work with an existing database.. 132
Select data from a single table 132
Select data from multiple tables.. 134
Insert, update, and delete data 135
Create other types of queries 138
Create transactions.. 139

Create a new database 140
Generate a script that creates a database 140
Run the script and test the database... 141

Perspective.. 142

How to work with SQLite

Before you can use Copilot to work with a SQLite database, you need to have some basic skills for working with a SQLite database. For example, you need to be able to run a SQL statement against a SQLite database to test any SQL that's generated by Copilot. To do that, we recommend using a program called DB Browser for SQLite.

Install DB Browser for SQLite

To install DB Browser for SQLite, you can use the following procedure.

How to install DB Browser for SQLite

1. Find the download page for DB Browser for SQLite by searching the internet for "DB Browser for SQLite".
2. Download the installer file.
3. Run the installer file and accept the default options when prompted.

Open a database and view its tables

Once you've installed DB Browser and started it, you can open a database by clicking the Open Database button. Then, you can use the resulting dialog to select the file for the database, which typically has a suffix of .db or .sqlite.

When you open a database, DB Browser displays the tables and indices for the database in the Database Structure tab as shown next.

The Database Structure tab

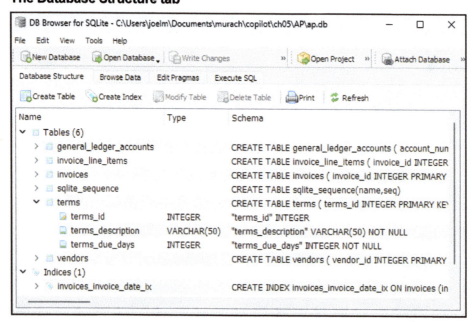

This Database Structure tab shows six tables and one index of a database for an Accounts Payable (AP) system. These tables store information about the vendors, invoices, line items, general ledger accounts, and payment terms. Most of the examples in this chapter use this database, and it's included in the download for this book. It's stored in a file named ap.db.

From the Database Structure tab, you can expand a table to display its columns and their data types. For example, the previous Database Structure tab shows the columns and data types for a table named terms.

If you want to view the data for a table, you can click the Browse Data tab. When you do, DB Browser displays the data for the selected table as shown next. This allows you to view all of the data in a table.

The Browse Data tab

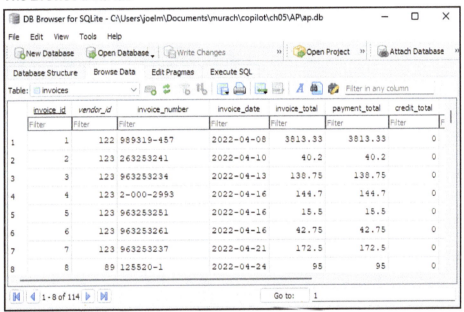

In this Browse Data tab, the invoices table is selected, and the tab shows data about invoices such as the invoice number, date, total, payment amount, and credit amount. Then, you can scroll to view more columns or more rows. Or, you can use the Table drop-down list to select any table in the database. For example, you can select the terms table to view data about payment terms.

In addition, you can filter the rows that are displayed by entering text in the box that displays just below each column name. For example, you could enter 100 in the invoice_id column to view the invoice with the id of 100.

Run SQL statements

When you use Copilot to generate SQL (Structured Query Language) statements, also known as *queries*, you can use DB Browser to run those SQL statements. This provides a way to test the query to make sure it does what you want. To do that, you can use the procedure shown here:

How to run SQL statements

1. Click the Execute SQL tab.
2. Enter the SQL statements into the code editor.
3. Click the Run button or press Ctrl+R (Windows) or Cmd+R (macOS).

For example, the Execute SQL tab shown next shows what DB Browser looks like after I ran a query that selected three columns from the invoices table.

A query after it has run in DB Browser

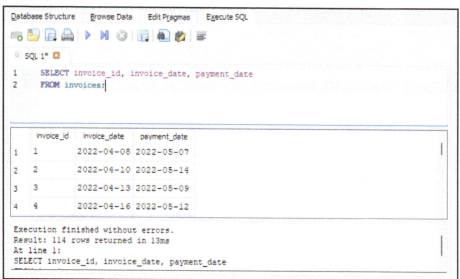

Here, the result set is displayed in a grid under the code editor. Beneath that, DB Browser displays another window that provides information about the query and any errors that it may have encountered. In this case, the query executed successfully, and it returned 114 rows.

In the previous example, the code editor only contains one SQL statement. However, you can enter multiple SQL statements. When you have multiple SQL statements in the code editor, you can click the Run button to run all of the SQL statements. But, if you only want to run one of those statements, you can select the statement you want to run and then click the Run button.

If you want to save SQL statements in a file, you can click the Save button. By default, this stores file with an extension of .sql.

Export a schema

To be able to use Copilot to generate SQL statements, you need to add context about the database to the prompt. In particular, Copilot needs to know how the tables and columns of the database are structured and related. To add this context, you can use DB Browser to export the schema for the database and store it in a file by using the following instructions.

How to export a schema

1. In DB Browser, select File ▶ Export ▶ Database to SQL file...
2. In the first drop-down, select "Export schema only".
3. Click Save and use the resulting dialog to save the file.

For example, I used these instructions to create a schema file for the AP database, and I stored it in a file named ap.schema.sql. The beginning of this file is shown next.

An excerpt from the schema file for the AP database

```sql
BEGIN TRANSACTION;
CREATE TABLE IF NOT EXISTS "general_ledger_accounts" (
    "account_number"      INTEGER,
    "account_description"   VARCHAR(50) UNIQUE,
    PRIMARY KEY("account_number")
);
CREATE TABLE IF NOT EXISTS "invoice_line_items" (
    "invoice_id"     INTEGER NOT NULL,
    "invoice_sequence"  INTEGER NOT NULL,
    "account_number"     INTEGER NOT NULL,
    "line_item_amount"  DECIMAL(9, 2) NOT NULL,
    "line_item_description" VARCHAR(100) NOT NULL,
    PRIMARY KEY("invoice_id","invoice_sequence"),
    FOREIGN KEY("account_number")
        REFERENCES "general_ledger_accounts"("account_number"),
    FOREIGN KEY("invoice_id")
        REFERENCES "invoices"("invoice_id")
);
CREATE TABLE IF NOT EXISTS "invoices" (
    "invoice_id"     INTEGER,
    "vendor_id" INTEGER NOT NULL,
...
```

This file contains multiple SQL statements that can be used to create the structure of the AP database. This provides context that Copilot needs to understand this database.

Work with an existing database

Now that you know the basics of using DB Browser to work with a SQLite database, you're ready to learn how to use Copilot to generate SQL statements that work with an existing database. To illustrate, this chapter shows how to generate SQL statements that work with the AP database.

Select data from a single table

Before you attempt to generate a query, you should add the schema file to the context for the prompt. For example, before I entered the following prompt, I opened the schema file for the AP database in the code editor. This added the schema file to the context for the prompt. Then, I specified the columns to return and a condition that specifies the rows to return.

A prompt that gets invoices that haven't been paid yet

In this prompt, I didn't provide the exact column names (I left out the underscores and shortened some column names), and I didn't explicitly specify the name of the table. Still, with the schema information as context, Copilot was able to determine the names of the columns, and it generated the following query. Since adding the schema file is so helpful, I made sure to add this file to the context for all prompts that work with the AP database throughout this chapter.

The generated query

```sql
SELECT invoice_id, invoice_date, payment_dat    Copy
FROM invoices
WHERE payment_date IS NULL;
```

When I reviewed the generated query, I was pleased to find that it included the correct columns, identified the correct table, and seemed to filter the rows correctly.

To test this query, I clicked the Copy icon above the suggested code and pasted it into DB Browser's Execute SQL tab. Then, I clicked the Run button, and DB Browser displayed a result set and some messages as shown next.

The query being tested in DB Browser

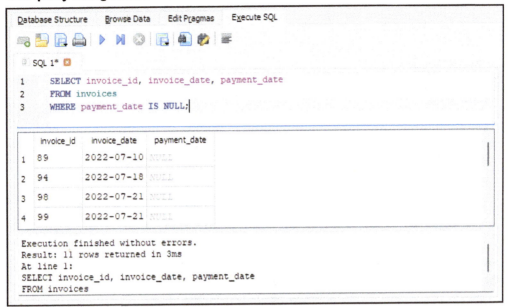

After reviewing the result set and execution messages, I determined that the generated query returned the correct data. In particular, since a paid invoice would have a payment date, the NULL value stored in the payment_date column shows that the result set contains unpaid invoices.

I decided that I wanted to modify this query, so I entered this prompt:

A prompt that modifies the previous query

Modify the previous query to sort the data in descending order based on the invoice_date column.

The generated query

```
SELECT invoice_id, invoice_date, payment_date
FROM invoices
WHERE payment_date IS NULL
ORDER BY invoice_date DESC;
```

When I reviewed the code for the generated query, it looked correct to me. Like the first query, I pasted it into DB Browser to test it, and I found that it correctly sorted the data in descending order by invoice date (most recent to least recent).

I was curious whether Copilot could filter for a range of dates, so I entered the following prompt.

A prompt that filters for a range of dates

> Create a query that returns the invoice id, date, and payment date for all invoices between 5/15/2022 and 6/15/2022.

The generated query

```
SELECT invoice_id, invoice_date, payment_date
FROM invoices
WHERE invoice_date BETWEEN '2022-05-15' AND '2022-06-15';
```

When I reviewed the generated query, I saw that Copilot used a BETWEEN clause to filter for data in a range. I also noticed that Copilot converted the date format in the prompt (MM/DD/YYYY) to the format required by SQLite (YYYY-MM-DD).

Select data from multiple tables

So far, the queries shown in this chapter have selected data from a single table. However, Copilot can also generate queries that select data from multiple tables. When you do this, you typically don't need to specify which tables to use if you supply the schema for the database as context for the prompt. In that case, Copilot can figure out how to connect the tables and retrieve the data on its own.

For example, to select data from the vendors and invoices tables, I entered the following prompt.

A prompt that asks for data from two tables

> Get the vendor name, invoice number, and invoice total for all invoices.

The generated query

```
SELECT vendors.vendor_name, invoices.invoice_number, invoices.invoice_total
FROM invoices
JOIN vendors ON invoices.vendor_id = vendors.vendor_id;
```

When I reviewed this query, I saw that it prefaced the name of each column with the name of the table. This works, but it's a common convention to use single-letter aliases for the table names because they make the code shorter and easier to read. Since I wanted to add these single-letter aliases, I entered the following prompt.

A prompt to create single-letter aliases for the table names

> Can you modify the previous query to use single-letter table aliases?

The generated query

```
SELECT v.vendor_name, i.invoice_number, i.invoice_total
FROM invoices i
JOIN vendors v ON i.vendor_id = v.vendor_id;
```

The query generated by Copilot used an inner join to join the two tables on the vendor_id column. As a result, this query only returns vendors that have invoices, not any vendors that don't at least one invoice.

However, I wanted to return all vendors, even if they don't have invoices, so I entered this prompt:

A prompt that queries data from two tables with an outer join

> Can you modify the previous query so it returns vendors even if they don't have an invoice?

The generated query

```
SELECT v.vendor_name, i.invoice_number, i.invoice_total
FROM vendors v
LEFT JOIN invoices i ON v.vendor_id = i.vendor_id;
```

This query uses a left outer join to join the tables on the vendor_id column. This means that the query returns all rows in the left (first) table but only matching rows from the right (second) table will be returned.

When using Copilot to create queries, the prompt can sometimes become longer than the query itself. That's because SQL is designed to succinctly describe a database operation. As a result, if you know SQL well, you may find it easier and more efficient to write the query in SQL rather than writing a prompt in English.

However, Copilot can still be helpful, especially if you're having trouble figuring out how to code a query. Also, if you add the schema for a database to the context, Copilot may suggest code that's helpful when you begin typing a query in the code editor. Then, if you want, you can accept that code by pressing Tab.

Insert, update, and delete data

Copilot can also be used to generate SQL statements that insert, update, or delete data. Before you run these statements, it's a good practice to back up your database. With a SQLite database, you can do this by making a copy of the database file, just like you would any other file.

If you want to insert a row into a table, you can generate a SQL statement to do that by entering a prompt like the one shown next. This prompt also asks Copilot to generate realistic data for the invoice.

A prompt that inserts a single row

> Add an invoice. Generate realistic data for this invoice.

The generated INSERT statement

```
INSERT INTO "invoices" (
    "vendor_id",
    "invoice_number",
```

```
        "invoice_date",
        "invoice_total",
        "payment_total",
        "credit_total",
        "terms_id",
        "invoice_due_date",
        "payment_date"
) VALUES (
    1, -- vendor_id
    'INV-2025-001', -- invoice_number
    '2025-03-14', -- invoice_date
    1500.00, -- invoice_total
    0.00, -- payment_total
    0.00, -- credit_total
    1, -- terms_id
    '2025-04-14', -- invoice_due_date
    NULL -- payment_date
);
```

Here, the generated statement includes double quotes around the table and column names. In addition, it includes comments to identify the column for each data value. These the double quotes and comments aren't necessary, and they cause the statement to use a lot of vertical space.

When I was done reviewing this statement, I decided that I didn't want the double quotes or comments because I wanted the INSERT statement to use less vertical space. So, I entered the following prompt to ask Copilot to modify the statement.

A prompt that modifies the INSERT statement

> Can you modify the previous statement to remove the double quotes and the comments so it takes less vertical space?

The modified INSERT statement

```
INSERT INTO invoices (
    vendor_id, invoice_number, invoice_date, invoice_total, payment_total,
    credit_total, terms_id, invoice_due_date, payment_date
) VALUES (
    1, 'INV-2025-001', '2025-03-14', 1500.00, 0.00, 0.00, 1, '2025-04-14', NULL
);
```

This code is more consistent with most coding standards and leaves out the unnecessary comments.

To test this statement, I copied it into DB Browser's SQL Execution tab and clicked the Run button. When I did that, DB Browser displayed the following message.

The message after running the INSERT statement

```
Execution finished without errors.
Result: query executed successfully. Took 11ms, 1 rows affected
```

This message indicates that the INSERT statement inserted the specified row. If I wanted, I could have verified this by using a SELECT statement to view the data for that row. However, I didn't do this because I felt confident that the statement executed correctly.

When you generate a statement that inserts, updates, or deletes data it's important to check the statement closely before running it. That's because these changes can't be easily undone, even if you have a backup.

You can also use Copilot to generate statements that insert multiple rows. For example, to insert three rows, I entered the prompt shown next.

A prompt for inserting multiple rows

Create a statement that inserts three invoices.
Generate realistic data for these invoices.

The generated INSERT statement

```
INSERT INTO invoices (
    vendor_id, invoice_number, invoice_date, invoice_total, payment_total,
    credit_total, terms_id, invoice_due_date, payment_date
) VALUES
    (1, 'INV-2025-002', '2025-03-27', 1200.00, 0.00, 0.00, 2, '2025-04-26', NULL),
    (2, 'INV-2025-003', '2025-03-25', 850.50, 0.00, 0.00, 3, '2025-04-24', NULL),
    (3, 'INV-2025-004', '2025-03-20', 450.75, 0.00, 0.00, 1, '2025-04-19', NULL);
```

Here, the generated INSERT statement is similar to the previous INSERT statement, except that it adds three rows of data instead of just one. When I tested this statement, DB Browser displayed a message that said 3 rows were affected, so I was confident that it worked correctly.

As you might expect, you can also use Copilot to generate UPDATE and DELETE statements as shown by the following prompts and responses.

A prompt that updates data

Update invoice 97/522 by increasing its credit total by 100.

The generated UPDATE statement

```
UPDATE invoices
SET credit_total = credit_total + 100
WHERE invoice_number = '97/522';
```

When testing an UPDATE statement, you can make sure it's going to update the correct rows by running a SELECT statement with the same WHERE clause. Then, once you're sure that the WHERE clause selects the correct rows, you can run the UPDATE statement.

When I tested this UPDATE statement, DB Browser displayed a message that said 1 row was affected. That makes sense as each invoice number should be unique.

A prompt that deletes data

Delete all line items with an invoice id of 12.

The generated DELETE statement

```
DELETE FROM invoice_line_items
WHERE invoice_id = 12;
```

The same techniques for testing an UPDATE statement can be applied to testing a DELETE statement. When I tested this DELETE statement, DB Browser displayed a message that said 1 row was affected. That makes sense as many invoices in this database only have one line item.

Create other types of queries

Copilot can help you generate all types of queries. For example, I entered the following prompt to generate a summary query.

A prompt for grouping and summarizing data

Get the vendor name and average invoice amount for each vendor that has an average invoice amount greater than $2000.

The generated query

```
SELECT v.vendor_name, AVG(i.invoice_total) AS average_invoice_amount
FROM invoices i
JOIN vendors v
ON i.vendor_id = v.vendor_id
GROUP BY v.vendor_name
HAVING AVG(i.invoice_total) > 2000;
```

Similarly, I entered the following prompt to generate another query. As it turned out, this query happens to use a subquery.

A prompt for a query that uses a subquery

Get the invoice number, date, and total for invoices with a total that's less than the average total for all invoices.

The generated query

```
SELECT invoice_number, invoice_date, invoice_total
FROM invoices
WHERE invoice_total < (SELECT AVG(invoice_total) FROM invoices);
```

To test a query that uses a subquery, it's sometimes helpful to test the subquery by running it separately. For example, with the previous query, I ran the subquery that gets the average invoices total to test whether it actually returns the average total for all invoices.

Create transactions

You can also use Copilot to generate a transaction that includes multiple INSERT, UPDATE, or DELETE statements that need to succeed or fail together. For example, when you delete an invoice, you need to delete the line items for the invoice as well. If your code for deleting the invoice fails, then the code for deleting the line items should fail too.

To create a transaction, you just need to tell Copilot that the operations need to take place within a transaction. For example, I entered the following prompt to create a transaction that deletes all invoices and invoice line items for a specified vendor.

A prompt that creates a transaction

Create a transaction that deletes all invoices and line items for vendor id 115.

The generated transaction

```
BEGIN TRANSACTION;

DELETE FROM invoice_line_items
WHERE invoice_id IN (
    SELECT invoice_id FROM invoices WHERE vendor_id = 115
);

DELETE FROM invoices
WHERE vendor_id = 115;

COMMIT;
```

The generated code adds the BEGIN TRANSACTION statement that starts the transaction and the COMMIT statement that ends it. Within these statements, the transaction includes two delete statements that delete the line items and invoices for the specified vendor. This looked correct to me, and when I ran the code, DB Browser displayed messages indicating that the code had executed successfully.

Create a new database

Now that you know how to use Copilot to work with an existing database, you're ready to learn how to use Copilot to create a new database. For instance, let's say you need to create a database from data that's stored in another standard format such as the comma-separated values (CSV) format like the one shown next. In that case, Copilot can help you design the database, and it can write the code that creates the database and stores the specified data.

The movies.csv file

```
name,year,minutes,category
Spirit: Stallion of the Cimarron,2002,83,Animation
Spirited Away,2001,125,Animation
Aladdin,1992,90,Animation
Ice Age,2002,81,Animation
Toy Story,1995,81,Animation
Monty Python and the Holy Grail,1975,91,Comedy
Monty Python's Life of Brian,1979,94,Comedy
Monty Python's The Meaning of Life,1983,107,Comedy
Gandhi,1982,191,History
Jinnah,1998,110,History
Lawrence of Arabia,1962,216,History
Hotel Rwanda,2004,121,History
Twelve Years a Slave,2013,134,History
```

In this CSV file, the first line specifies the names for the four columns. Then, the next 13 lines store the data for each movie. In this data, the fourth column specifies the category for each movie. Since the category column contains duplicate values, this data structure isn't normalized.

Generate a script that creates a database

To create the database for the movies.csv file, I entered the following prompt. But first, I added the movies.csv file to the context for the prompt. To do that, I right-clicked on the movies.csv file in VS Code's Explorer and selected Copilot ▶ Add File to Chat.

A prompt that creates a database

Create a normalized SQLite database that stores the data in the movies.csv file.

Within this prompt, I asked Copilot to normalize the data. I did that because I didn't want Copilot to create a database that stored all of the data in a single table. Instead, I wanted Copilot to create a script for two related tables.

The generated script

```sql
BEGIN TRANSACTION;

CREATE TABLE categories (
    category_id INTEGER PRIMARY KEY AUTOINCREMENT,
    category_name VARCHAR(50) NOT NULL UNIQUE
);

CREATE TABLE movies (
    movie_id INTEGER PRIMARY KEY AUTOINCREMENT,
    name VARCHAR(100) NOT NULL,
    year INTEGER NOT NULL,
    minutes INTEGER NOT NULL,
    category_id INTEGER NOT NULL,
    FOREIGN KEY (category_id) REFERENCES categories (category_id)
);

INSERT INTO categories (category_name) VALUES
    ('Animation'),
    ('Comedy'),
    ('History');

INSERT INTO movies (name, year, minutes, category_id) VALUES
    ('Spirit: Stallion of the Cimarron', 2002, 83, 1),
    ('Spirited Away', 2001, 125, 1),
    ('Aladdin', 1992, 90, 1),
    ('Ice Age', 2002, 81, 1),
    ('Toy Story', 1995, 81, 1),
    ('Monty Python and the Holy Grail', 1975, 91, 2),
    ('Monty Python''s Life of Brian', 1979, 94, 2),
    ('Monty Python''s The Meaning of Life', 1983, 107, 2),
    ('Gandhi', 1982, 191, 3),
    ('Jinnah', 1998, 110, 3),
    ('Lawrence of Arabia', 1962, 216, 3),
    ('Hotel Rwanda', 2004, 121, 3),
    ('Twelve Years a Slave', 2013, 134, 3);

COMMIT;
```

When I reviewed this script, it looked like it should create the database I want, so I saved it with a name of create_movies_db.sql.

Run the script and test the database

Before you can run a script to create a database, you need to use DB Browser to create a blank database file. To do that, click the New Database button and enter a name for the database such as movies.db. You don't need to create any of the tables, so if DB Browser prompts you to edit table definitions, click Cancel. When you're done, you should have a file for a blank database.

With a blank database file open, you can run the script to create the database. If the script runs successfully, it should create the tables and insert the data. To test this, you can switch to the Browse Data tab, click the Refresh icon, and select the table you want to view as shown next.

The movies table in the Browse Data tab

On the other hand, if the script doesn't execute successfully, you can ask Copilot to fix the script. If you're getting an error message, you can include that message in the prompt to give Copilot more context for the error.

Perspective

This chapter started by showing how to use Copilot to generate SQL that works with an existing database. Then, it showed how to use Copilot to generate SQL that creates a new database. Although the databases shown in this chapter are simpler than most databases in the real world, you can use the same techniques to generate SQL for working with more complex databases.

Exercises

1. Generate SQL that returns every vendor with the contact information for that vendor.

2. Generate SQL that adds a new invoice that has three line items. This invoice should have realistic data.

3. Generate SQL that creates tables for a small book management system. You should include a books table and an authors table that are linked together by a foreign key. Once you've created the tables, you should generate SQL code to insert some data into each table.

Chapter 6

Design and maintain software

The software development process can vary widely between different organizations, but it typically includes planning, designing, implementing, testing, deploying, and maintaining the software. So far, this book has focused on showing how to implement software with some minimal testing. However, you can use Copilot in all phases of software development, and this chapter shows some ways you can use Copilot for planning, designing, and maintaining software.

To illustrate how you can use Copilot to help with these phases of software development, this chapter mostly uses Python. However, the concepts and skills presented in this chapter apply to most programming languages.

How to design new software 144
Gather requirements 144
Make architectural decisions 151
Create a project structure 154
Address other planning issues 156

How to maintain existing software 157
Analyze existing code 157
Find and fix bugs 159
Find and fix security issues 160
Add comments 162
Create a README.md file 163

Perspective 166

How to design new software

Copilot can help you plan and design new software. For example, you can use Copilot to help you gather requirements for a system, to help you decide which tools to use to implement the requirements, and so on.

Gather requirements

Gathering the requirements for a project can be crucial for success. Often, this involves asking the users of the proposed software questions and then translating what they want into software that meets their needs. However, users are often unsure of exactly what they need or they may forget details, and it can often be difficult to determine all of the details before you start coding. Fortunately, Copilot can help you by generating ideas, follow-up questions, and additional considerations that you might overlook otherwise.

For example, if you want to create a program that stores data about movies, you could open a Chat window and enter the following prompt.

A prompt for identifying the data for a Movies program

> I want to create a program that stores information about movies and puts them into categories. What kind of data should I consider storing to represent a movie? What kind of categories can I divide movies into?

When I entered this prompt, Copilot gave me the following response.

A response that identifies some data for a Movies program

 GitHub Copilot

> Used 1 reference

To represent a movie, you should consider storing the following data:

1. **Title**: The name of the movie.
2. **Director**: The person who directed the movie.
3. **Release Year**: The year the movie was released.
4. **Genre**: The category or categories the movie falls into (e.g., Action, Comedy).
5. **Cast**: The main actors and actresses in the movie.
6. **Rating**: The movie's rating (e.g., PG, R).
7. **Duration**: The length of the movie in minutes.
8. **Synopsis**: A brief summary of the movie's plot.
9. **Language**: The language(s) spoken in the movie.
10. **Country**: The country where the movie was produced.

This response started by listing ten types of data. Then, it included information about different genres to consider. In addition, it included the code for a Python class that could be used to store this data.

In this case, I thought Python was a good choice, so I decided to use it for the rest of this chapter. However, Copilot might not always suggest a language, and it might not always suggest Python.

When you ask Copilot for ideas about what data to store, you might want to store more or less data than it suggests. However, the suggestions provide a good starting point for gathering the requirements for this program.

In this case, I decided that I wanted to limit the data for the program to the movie's title, release year, genre, and duration. To do that, I entered the following prompt.

A prompt that specifies the data to use

I want to create a simple program that only stores title, release year, genre, and duration.

When I entered this prompt, Copilot adjusted the context for the chat accordingly.

For the Movies program, I decided that I wanted to use a command-line interface (CLI). To determine how that interface might look before I began coding, I entered a prompt like the one shown next.

A prompt for mocking up the user interface

I want to use a command line interface for this program. Can you show me how this interface might look to a user?

When I entered this prompt, I got the following response.

A response that includes a mockup of a user interface

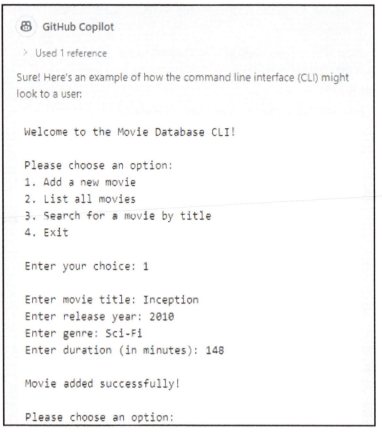

GitHub Copilot

> Used 1 reference

Sure! Here's an example of how the command line interface (CLI) might look to a user:

```
Welcome to the Movie Database CLI!

Please choose an option:
1. Add a new movie
2. List all movies
3. Search for a movie by title
4. Exit

Enter your choice: 1

Enter movie title: Inception
Enter release year: 2010
Enter genre: Sci-Fi
Enter duration (in minutes): 148

Movie added successfully!

Please choose an option:
```

This response included a menu that allows the user to enter a number to select the options for using the program. In addition, it provided usage examples for several of these options. This should give you a good starting point for how this interface could work. Then, you can determine ways to modify the user interface to customize it and improve it for your purposes.

Note that the prompt and the response for mocking up the user interface use the previous prompts and responses as context. As a result, the interface only works with the movie title, year, genre, and duration.

When you're planning software, it often makes sense to create a *requirements document*, which is a document that contains a list of requirements for the software. This document can be a valuable resource for making sure the programmers have agreed on what the software should do. Then, programmers might be able to use the requirements document to help craft prompts for generating the code for a program.

To create a requirements document, you can enter a prompt like the one shown next.

A prompt that starts a requirements document

Can you create a requirements document for the discussed Movies program?

When I entered this prompt, I got the following response.

A response with the generated document

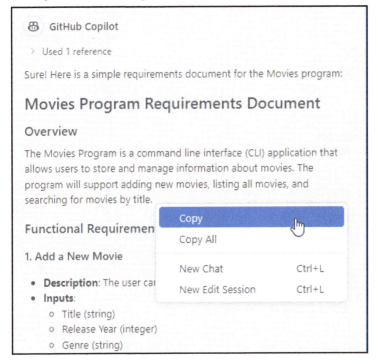

This response included functional requirements, non-functional requirements, and information about the user interface, including example usage. In addition, it included information about data storage. To get this document out of the Chat window and into a text file, I used the following steps.

How to copy a response into a text file

1. Right-click the response and select Copy.
2. Select File ▶ New Text File to open a new text file in the code editor.
3. Paste the response into the blank file in the code editor.
4. Save the file with an extension of .md.

When I pasted the response into the code editor, it contained *markdown*, which is a language that provides structure and formatting for the content of a document as shown next.

The markdown for the generated document

```
# Movies Program Requirements Document

## Overview
The Movies Program is a command line interface (CLI) application that allows users to
store and manage information about movies. The program will support adding new movies,
listing all movies, and searching for movies by title.

## Functional Requirements

### 1. Add a New Movie
- **Description**: The user can add a new movie to the database.
- **Inputs**:
  - Title (string)
  - Release Year (integer)
  - Genre (string)
  - Duration (integer, in minutes)
- **Outputs**: Confirmation message indicating the movie was added successfully.

### 2. List All Movies
- **Description**: The user can list all movies stored in the database.
- **Inputs**: None
- **Outputs**: A list of all movies with the following details:
  - Title
  - Release Year
  - Genre
  - Duration

### 3. Search for a Movie by Title
- **Description**: The user can search for a movie by its title.
- **Inputs**:
  - Title (string)
- **Outputs**: Details of the movie matching the title, if found:
  - Title
  - Release Year
  - Genre
  - Duration
  - If no movie is found, an appropriate message is displayed.

### 4. Exit the Program
- **Description**: The user can exit the program.
- **Inputs**: None
- **Outputs**: A goodbye message.

## Non-Functional Requirements

### 1. Usability
- The program should be easy to use with clear prompts and messages.

### 2. Performance
- The program should handle a reasonable number of movies without significant
performance degradation.

### 3. Portability
- The program should run on any system with Python installed.

## User Interface
```

```
### Command Line Interface (CLI)
- The program will interact with the user through a text-based command line
interface.
- The user will be presented with a menu of options to choose from.

## Example User Interaction
(Not shown here to save space)

## Data Storage
- The program will store movie data in memory for the duration of the session.
- Persistent storage is not required for this version of the program.
```

This markdown uses a single hash mark (#) to identify a level-1 heading, two hash marks (##) for level-2 headings, three hash marks (###) for level-3 headings, indentation along with a hyphen (-) to identify bullets, and double asterisks (**) to identify bold text.

VS Code provides functionality to help you navigate and preview markdown code. To preview the markdown code, you can right-click on the markdown file in the Explorer window and select Open Preview. This opens the markdown file in Preview mode as shown next.

The requirements.md file in Preview mode

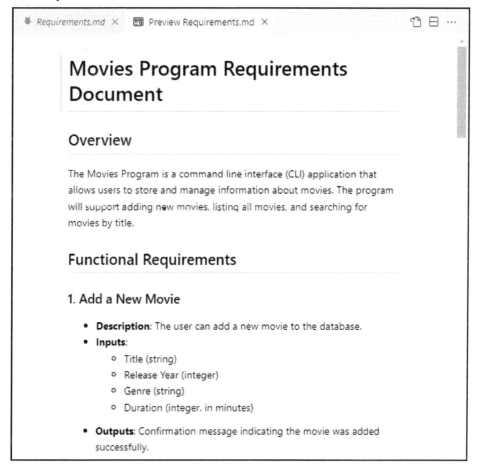

In addition to previewing the markdown, you can also use the Outline view to quickly navigate within the markdown file. To open this view, open the markdown file in the code editor and expand the Outline view in the Explorer window as shown next.

The Outline view open in the Explorer window

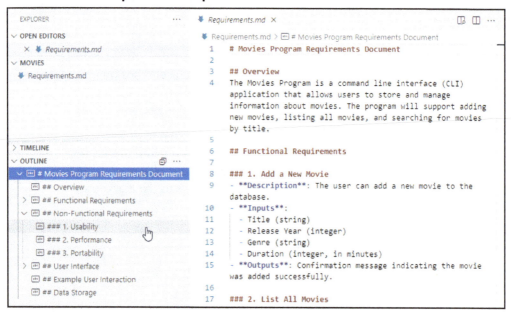

Once you expand the Outline view, you can click on any of the headings to navigate to that heading in the code editor.

In this requirements document, the Portability section indicates that the program should run on any system that has Python installed. When you're planning software, you might not need to decide what language to use just yet. Instead, you can focus on what the code needs to do to satisfy the client and decide on the language later. On the other hand, you or your client might specify the language to use. If so, you can modify the requirements document to specify the language that you plan to use. For now, I decided to leave the requirements document as is with Python as the specified language.

If you generate a requirements document, you can use it as a starting point. Then, you can modify the requirements to meet the needs of your software. Or, you can continue your chat to use Copilot to further refine the requirements.

For large software projects, you may want to split your requirements document into separate documents for each component of your system. This makes each document easier to maintain. For example, you may have one requirements document for a program that's used by your client and another for an API that provides data to the program.

Make architectural decisions

Once you've gathered the requirements for your software, Copilot can help make the design decisions that form the foundation of your software. These decisions can be high-level decisions like the architecture of the entire system or they can be lower-level suggestions like which frameworks to use and how to structure your data. To make these decisions, it's often helpful to provide a well-defined requirements document to Copilot as context.

When choosing technologies to use in your projects, Copilot can provide valuable information to help you make informed decisions. For example, based on your requirements documents, Copilot can recommend programming languages, frameworks, libraries, modules, databases, or API design patterns that would work well for your project.

For the Movies program, I decided to use Python as the programming language and that information is already in the requirements document. However, I hadn't decided on a database system yet. To help me decide which database would be optimal for this program, I added the requirements document to the context for the Chat window. Then, I entered the following prompt:

A prompt for getting recommendations for database systems

> Recommend three database technologies for the Movies program and compare and contrast them.

Recommendations for database systems

 GitHub Copilot

Sure! Here are three database technologies you can consider for storing information about movies in your Python program:

1. **SQLite**
2. **PostgreSQL**
3. **MongoDB**

SQLite

Pros:

- **Lightweight and Serverless:** SQLite is a self-contained, serverless database engine, making it easy to set up and use.
- **Zero Configuration:** No setup or administration required, which is ideal for small applications or development environments.
- **File-Based:** Stores the entire database in a single file, making it easy to manage and distribute.

Cons:

- **Limited Scalability:** Not suitable for high-concurrency or large-scale applications.
- **Fewer Features:** Lacks some advanced features found in other RDBMS like PostgreSQL.
- **Concurrency:** Limited support for concurrent writes.

This response provided the pros and cons for three database systems. Based on this information, I decided to use SQLite for this program.

A prompt for identifying the classes

I have decided to use SQLite as the database, and I want to normalize the data. What classes would you use to store the data for the movie?

In this prompt, it's important to include the word *normalize*. That's because relational databases like SQLite can use data normalization to structure data in a way that reduces redundancy, improves data integrity, and enhances query efficiency.

A response that suggests how to structure the classes

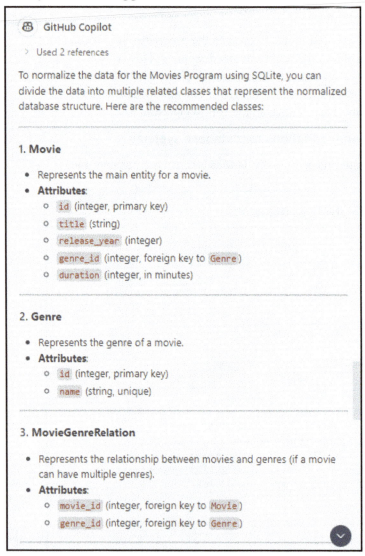

⊞ GitHub Copilot

> Used 2 references

To normalize the data for the Movies Program using SQLite, you can divide the data into multiple related classes that represent the normalized database structure. Here are the recommended classes:

1. Movie

- Represents the main entity for a movie.
- **Attributes:**
    - `id` (integer, primary key)
    - `title` (string)
    - `release_year` (integer)
    - `genre_id` (integer, foreign key to `Genre`)
    - `duration` (integer, in minutes)

2. Genre

- Represents the genre of a movie.
- **Attributes:**
    - `id` (integer, primary key)
    - `name` (string, unique)

3. MovieGenreRelation

- Represents the relationship between movies and genres (if a movie can have multiple genres).
- **Attributes:**
    - `movie_id` (integer, foreign key to `Movie`)
    - `genre_id` (integer, foreign key to `Genre`)

This response started by recommending some classes. Then, it explained normalization, provided code for creating the database tables, and provided code for the classes. This information provided a good starting point for deciding how to use classes to store the data for this program.

You can also use Copilot to critique any architectural decisions that you've made. Sometimes asking for a critique can reveal oversights, better options, or design improvements in your architecture. Catching these issues early can save you time later. For example, to get a critique of the architecture that I was planning to use for the Movies program, I entered the following prompt.

A prompt that asks for a critique of the architecture

For the Movies program, I'm planning to use this architecture:

Frontend: Command line interface
Backend: Python
Database: SQLite

Can you identify potential bottlenecks?

When I sent this prompt to Copilot, it returned the following response.

A response that identifies some potential bottlenecks

Potential Bottlenecks

1. **Database Query Performance**
   - If the database grows significantly, queries like searching for a movie by title or listing all movies could slow down.
   - **Mitigation**: Add appropriate indexes (e.g., on the `title` column) to improve query performance.
2. **Concurrency**
   - SQLite is not designed for high-concurrency environments. If multiple users or processes attempt to access the database simultaneously, it could lead to locking issues.
   - **Mitigation**: Since this is a CLI program, concurrency is unlikely to be an issue. However, if needed, consider switching to a more robust database like PostgreSQL for multi-user scenarios.
3. **Data Validation**
   - If user input is not validated properly, invalid data (e.g., non-integer values for `release_year` or `duration`) could cause runtime errors or corrupt the database.
   - **Mitigation**: Implement strict input validation in the service layer.
4. **Scalability**
   - The program is designed for a single-user CLI interface. If the program needs to scale to a web or multi-user application, the architecture may need significant changes.
   - **Mitigation**: For now, this is acceptable for a CLI-based program.

For the simple Movies program that I'm planning on developing, some of these issues are relevant while others are not. For example, since I have no plans to scale this program to a web or multi-user application, concurrency and scalability aren't an issue. However, database query performance and data validation are relevant issues.

Here are a few more examples of how you can use Copilot to help you make architectural decisions for your programs. If you run these prompts, I think you'll see that they provide useful info.

A prompt that gets software suggestions based on the type of license

I'm writing some proprietary software that needs to use an RDBMS system. Can you find a RDBMS system that has a license that doesn't mandate that I open source my code?

A prompt that gets software suggestions based on needed features

I'm trying to choose a database for a website that I'm developing. The database will need to store text data initially but may need to accommodate PDF and image data in the future. Recommend several systems that can accommodate this and compare them.

A prompt that gets suggestions for alternative software

I'm writing a website with Django and I'm now starting to implement asynchronous code. However, Django's default development server doesn't support asynchronous code. Can you recommend an alternative development server?

Create a project structure

Copilot can help create file structures for your project, especially if you're using a new framework or technology. However, Copilot doesn't always make the best decisions. As a result, you need to be the final judge of whether a file structure generated by Copilot works correctly for your project.

To create a file structure for the Movies program, I entered the following prompt.

A prompt for determining the file structure of the Movie List app

For the Movies program, I'd like to use a three-tier architecture to separate the user interface, model, and database layers. How would you recommend structuring the files for this program?

A response that includes a recommended file structure

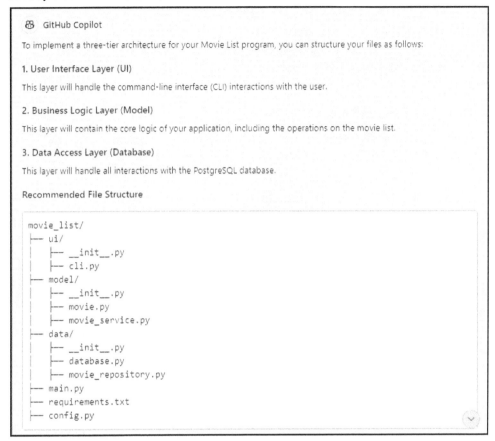

GitHub Copilot

To implement a three-tier architecture for your Movie List program, you can structure your files as follows:

1. User Interface Layer (UI)

This layer will handle the command-line interface (CLI) interactions with the user.

2. Business Logic Layer (Model)

This layer will contain the core logic of your application, including the operations on the movie list.

3. Data Access Layer (Database)

This layer will handle all interactions with the PostgreSQL database.

Recommended File Structure

```
movie_list/
├── ui/
│   ├── __init__.py
│   ├── cli.py
├── model/
│   ├── __init__.py
│   ├── movie.py
│   ├── movie_service.py
├── data/
│   ├── __init__.py
│   ├── database.py
│   ├── movie_repository.py
├── main.py
├── requirements.txt
├── config.py
```

This recommended a file structure that places each component into its own directory. This structure looked reasonable to me, but I thought it included more files than I needed.

To start, I didn't think I would need the __init__.py files. These files help identify a directory as a package, but they're only required prior to Python version 3.2. In addition, the model and data directories each contained two files, but I thought I would only need one per directory. Finally, I didn't think I would need the config.py or requirements.txt files. Still, it's easy to delete files, so I thought this directory structure would make a good enough starting point for the Movies program.

Address other planning issues

When you're developing software, there are many other issues you may encounter when planning and designing your software. If you want, you can ask Copilot to help you address these issues, as shown by the following prompts.

A prompt to help you start a group project

> I am a beginning programmer who is starting a group programming project for the first time. What are some things that I can do to help this group work together effectively?

When I entered this prompt, the response provided a variety of helpful information about programming in teams. This included information about technology that can be used to help with group programming such as version control and project management software as well as information about best practices like adopting a consistent coding style and breaking up work among different team members.

You can also use Copilot to expand on information that it's already given. For example, the previous prompt recommended using GitHub for version control. If you want more information about this topic, you can use the following prompts to get a more in-depth explanation

A prompt that asks for an example of version control

> I am working on a group project with some programmers who are learning to use version control for the first time. Can you give a basic example of how we might use GitHub for version control?

If you're working with a group of programmers, you may need help dividing, assigning, and scheduling work. Fortunately, Copilot can help with that. For example, the following prompt asks for help with dividing the work for the week. In cases like this, you can often make a better judgment than Copilot. Still, it's often helpful to get ideas from Copilot first.

A prompt to help you divide and assign work

> I am working with two other programmers on a software project and we need help dividing up the work that needs to be done. I have attached a text file that details the tasks that need to be accomplished this week.

Selecting the technologies to use in a project can also affect the way you work. It can be tempting to stick with what you know since that may seem easier. However, choosing to learn a new framework or language can be a great opportunity to grow as a programmer and may be easier than you think. To gauge the difficulty of using an unfamiliar technology in your project, you can enter a prompt like the one shown next.

A prompt to help you gauge the difficulty of using a new language

> I've been programming in C++ for a year. I'm working on a project that I have four weeks to complete and I have the option to use another language. Would it be realistic for me to learn and use Python to implement this project instead of C++ within this timeframe?

If you enter this prompt, Copilot will respond with an estimate of the difficulty and if it thinks this is a realistic goal. However, Copilot can be overly optimistic, so it may be better to ask Copilot what you would need to learn to accomplish a project. Then, you can make your own time estimate.

How to maintain existing software

When you maintain software, you might fix bugs, address customer concerns, improve code quality, and add documentation. But first, if you're unfamiliar with the software, you may need to analyze it to help you understand it.

To illustrate, the headings that follow show how to maintain the Movie List program that's included in the download for this book. This program uses the following file structure.

The starting files for a Movie List program

Here, the three Python files provide the code for the program, and the program stores the data in a SQLite database named movies.sqlite.

Analyze existing code

Software development often involves building on an existing codebase. In that case, a developer needs to understand the existing codebase well enough to be able to build on it. This can be a time-consuming part of the process. Fortunately, Copilot can help you get up to speed.

For example, you can ask Copilot to summarize the main components of a codebase and to explain how they work together. This can help you to determine where you need to put new code within the existing codebase.

Before you summarize code files, you need to add them to the context for the Chat window. For example, I added all three of the files for the Movie List program to the context for the following prompt. Then, I asked Copilot to summarize these files.

A prompt that summarizes some code files

The end of the response that summarizes the files

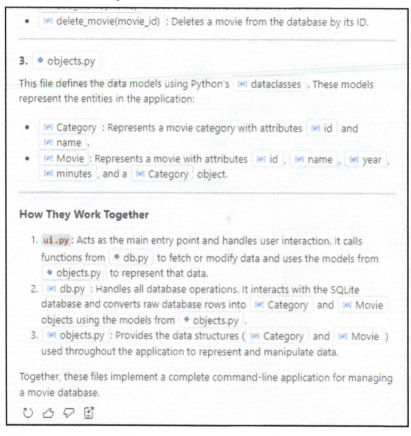

- delete_movie(movie_id) : Deletes a movie from the database by its ID.

3. objects.py

This file defines the data models using Python's dataclasses . These models represent the entities in the application:

- Category : Represents a movie category with attributes id and name .
- Movie : Represents a movie with attributes id , name , year , minutes , and a Category object.

How They Work Together

1. ui.py : Acts as the main entry point and handles user interaction. It calls functions from db.py to fetch or modify data and uses the models from objects.py to represent that data.
2. db.py : Handles all database operations. It interacts with the SQLite database and converts raw database rows into Category and Movie objects using the models from objects.py .
3. objects.py : Provides the data structures (Category and Movie) used throughout the application to represent and manipulate data.

Together, these files implement a complete command-line application for managing a movie database.

This response started by summarizing the functions and classes provided by each of the specified files. Then, it finished with an explanation of how the files work together. If you're new to a codebase, a summary like this one can help you understand how the code works.

After reading a summary like the one shown previously, you may want more detail about a particular component. In that case, you can enter another prompt. For the Movie List program, you may want to enter one of the following prompts.

A prompt that asks for information about an object

> What methods are available from the Movie class?

You can use a prompt like this to get more detailed information about a specific class.

A prompt that asks how two files are related

> How are the db.py and objects.py files related?

You can use a prompt like this to learn more about how two specific files are related. This can be helpful if one file imports another and you need to understand how the imported file is being used.

Find and fix bugs

Bugs are an inevitable part of developing software, and fixing them is a critical part of programming. If a bug displays an error message when it occurs, you can often use Copilot to help you fix the bug. To do that, copy the error message that's displayed in the Terminal and paste it into a prompt. Then, edit the prompt to ask for help fixing the bug.

For example, I introduced an error into the Movies List program by changing the name of the table in the get_categories() function from Category to Categories. Then, when I ran the program, the Terminal displayed an error message that ended like this:

The end of an error message displayed in the Terminal

```
File "...\movie_list\db.py", line 36, in get_categories
    c.execute(query)
sqlite3.OperationalError: no such table: Categories
```

To see if Copilot could help me fix this error, I added the db.py file to the context for the prompt. Then, I copied the error message from the Terminal, pasted it into the prompt, and asked for help fixing the bug as shown next.

A prompt for fixing a bug that has an error message

> I'm getting the following error message. Can you show me how to fix it?
>
> File "...\movie_list\db.py", line 36, in get_categories
>   c.execute(query)
> sqlite3.OperationalError: no such table: Categories

When I entered this prompt, Copilot gave me some useful information about this bug. However, the response made it clear that the Chat window didn't have information about the database structure in its context. As a result, it wasn't able to suggest a fix for the problem.

To give more context to Copilot for this issue, I created a schema file for the database as described in chapter 5. Then, I added the schema file to the context for the previous prompt and ran it again. This time, Copilot suggested the correct fix for this issue.

If a bug doesn't display an error message but still causes your program to perform incorrectly, you can describe the problem in a prompt and provide any relevant code. If you provide the correct context, Copilot may be able to explain what's causing the bug, and it can often suggest code that will fix it. Even if Copilot can't fix the bug, it's likely to provide ideas that can stimulate your thoughts about how to fix it.

Find and fix security issues

Before software is deployed, it should be checked to make sure it doesn't have security vulnerabilities. However, after software is deployed, new security vulnerabilities may be discovered. When that happens, you need to modify the code to fix the security vulnerability. To do that, you can use Copilot to help you to identify and understand common security vulnerabilities.

To test this, I introduced a security vulnerability known as a SQL injection attack into the db.py file. To do that, I modified the code so it uses concatenation to add the category_id parameter to the end of the query as shown next.

A function in the db.py with a security vulnerability

```
def get_category_name(category_id):
    query = '''SELECT categoryID, name as categoryName FROM category
               WHERE categoryID = '''
    query += category_id
    with closing(connection.cursor()) as cursor:
        cursor.execute(query)
        row = cursor.fetchone()
        if row:
            return make_category(row)
        else:
            return None
```

Then, I entered the following prompt to see if Copilot could find this security issue.

A prompt to locate security issues

> Examine my db.py file and identify any security issues. If you identify any issues, explain them and suggest a fix for the issue.

When I sent this prompt to Copilot, it returned a response that identified three security issues, including the SQL injection vulnerability, and suggested fixes for all of them. For example, the response started with the following explanation of the SQL injection issue that I introduced earlier.

A response that explains a security issue

Security Issues in ✦ db.py

1. SQL Injection in `get_category`

- The `get_category` function concatenates `category_id` directly into the SQL query string:

```
query = '''SELECT categoryID, name AS categoryName
           FROM Category WHERE categoryID = '''
query += str(category_id)
```

- This approach is vulnerable to SQL injection if `category_id` is derived from user input.

In addition, it suggested the following fix for this issue:

A response that suggests a fix for a security issue

Fix: Use parameterized queries to prevent SQL injection.

```
def get_category(category_id):
    query = '''SELECT categoryID, name AS categoryName
               FROM Category WHERE categoryID = ?'''
    with closing(conn.cursor()) as c:
        c.execute(query, (category_id,))
        row = c.fetchone()
        if row:
            return make_category(row)
        else:
            return None
```

This fix looked good to me, so I hovered the mouse over the code and clicked the Apply icon. This displayed the suggested changes in the code editor window, and I accepted them.

After fixing this issue, I read through the other two issues in the response. First, the response said there was another potential SQL injection vulnerability in the add_movie() function and that its parameters should be sanitized, even though it uses parameterized queries. Second, the response said the close() function improperly handles the database connection in a way that could lead to errors.

After reviewing the code, I decided that neither issue was relevant to this program. As a result, I didn't fix either issue. This shows that it's important to review Copilot's suggestions and make your own decisions based on those suggestions.

Add comments

To have Copilot create comments that document each function in a file, you can use a simple prompt like the one next. But first, make sure to add the file or files to the context for the Chat window.

A prompt that adds comments to all functions

Add docstring comments to each function in the attached file.

When I used this prompt with the db.py file attached, Copilot generated docstring comments for every function in the file. For instance, for the get_categories() function, it generated this docstring comment:

A function in the db.py file with docstring comments

```python
def get_category(category_id):
    """
    Retrieve a category from the database based on the given category ID.

    Args:
        category_id (int): The ID of the category to retrieve.

    Returns:
        dict or None: A dictionary representing the category with keys
        'categoryID' and 'categoryName' if found, otherwise None.
    """
    query = '''SELECT categoryID, name AS categoryName
                FROM Category WHERE categoryID = ?'''
    with closing(conn.cursor()) as c:
        c.execute(query, (category_id,))
        row = c.fetchone()
        if row:
            return make_category(row)
        else:
            return None
```

When I reviewed these comments, I found that they were mostly correct. So, this saved me a lot of busywork!

However, I found a few places where I thought the comments could be improved. For example, the previous function returns an object, not a dict. So, I modified that part of the comment to make it more accurate.

If you only want to generate comments for specified functions, you have a couple options. First, you can use the Chat window to specify the function name in the prompt as shown next.

A prompt that adds docstring comments to a single function

Add docstring comments to the display_movies_by_category() function.

Or, you can select the function in the code editor, and use the inline chat interface to enter the /doc command as shown next.

An inline prompt with the /doc command for a single function

```
/doc Add documentation comment for this symbol          ⬛  🎤  GPT-4o ∨  ⤳ ∨

38   def get_int(prompt):
39        while True:
40            try:
41                return int(input(prompt))
42            except ValueError:
43                print("Invalid whole number. Please try again.\n")
44
```

When I tested both of these techniques, they both generated a docstring comment similar to the one shown next.

The function with a generated docstring comment

```
def get_int(prompt):
    """
    Prompt the user to input a whole number and validate the input.

    This function repeatedly prompts the user with the given message until a valid
    integer is entered. If the user enters an invalid value, an error message is
    displayed, and the prompt is shown again.

    Args:
        prompt (str): The message to display to the user when requesting input.

    Returns:
        int: The integer value entered by the user.
    """
    while True:
        try:
            return int(input(prompt))
        except ValueError:
            print("Invalid whole number. Please try again.\n")
```

Since this comment accurately documents the function, I didn't make any changes to it.

Create a README.md file

For many kinds of software, it's helpful to provide a document that gives an overview of how the software works. One way to do that is to create a README file. A *README file* typically provides general information about your project and what a user needs to do to run it. This documentation also makes it easy for other programmers to quickly get up to speed with your project.

To create a README file, it's common to use markdown to provide the structure and formatting for the document. Because of that, these files are often named README.md (the md is for markdown).

If you create a repository for your project with GitHub, it may automatically create a README.md file for your project. In that case, you can use Copilot to update this file to reflect the updated project. Otherwise, you can create a new README.md file.

To create a README.md file for the Movie List program, I added the three Python files for the program to the context for the Chat window and entered this prompt:

A prompt for creating a README.md file

Create a README.md file for the Movie List program.

When I ran this prompt, the response included this markdown:

The generated markdown

```
# Movie List Program

The **Movie List Program** is a Python-based application that allows users to manage a
list of movies stored in a SQLite database. Users can view movies by category or year,
add new movies, and delete existing ones. The program is designed to demonstrate basic
database operations and user interaction through a command-line interface.

---

## Features

- **View Movies by Category**: Display all movies belonging to a specific category.
- **View Movies by Year**: Display all movies released in a specific year.
- **Add a Movie**: Add a new movie to the database with details such as name, year,
duration, and category.
- **Delete a Movie**: Remove a movie from the database by its ID.
- **Category Management**: View a list of all available categories.

---

## Requirements

- Python 3.8 or higher
- SQLite3
- Required Python modules:
  - `sqlite3`
  - `dataclasses`

---

## File Structure

- **`db.py`**: Handles database operations such as connecting to the database, re-
trieving categories, and managing movies.
- **`ui.py`**: Provides the user interface and handles user input/output.
- **`objects.py`**: Defines the `Category` and `Movie` data classes.
- **`movies.sqlite.sql`**: SQL script to create the database schema.

---

## Database Schema

The program uses a SQLite database with the following schema:

### Tables
```

```
1. **Category**
   - `categoryID` (INTEGER, Primary Key)
   - `name` (TEXT, Not Null)

2. **Movie**
   - `movieID` (INTEGER, Primary Key)
   - `categoryID` (INTEGER, Foreign Key referencing `Category.categoryID`)
   - `name` (TEXT, Not Null)
   - `year` (INTEGER, Not Null)
   - `minutes` (INTEGER, Not Null)

---

## How to Run

1. Clone or download the repository to your local machine.
2. Ensure Python 3.8 or higher is installed.
3. Create the SQLite database by running the `movies.sqlite.sql` script:
   ```bash
   sqlite3 movies.sqlite < movies.sqlite.sql
```

This markdown describes this program, its features, its requirements, its database, and how to run the program. I was surprised that this markdown included info about the database, but I had included the database schema earlier in the chat, so it makes sense that Copilot would use it as part of the context for the chat.

When I reviewed this markdown, I thought it was a good starting point, so I saved it with a filename of README.md. Since the file for the SQLite database already exists, there's no need to create this file. So, I would edit the "How to Run" section to reflect that. Otherwise, I was satisfied with this markdown.

If you want to view the formatted result of the markdown, you can right-click on the README.md file in the Explorer window and select Open Preview. Then, VS Code uses the markdown tags to format the README file as shown next.
```

The beginning of the README.md file in Preview mode

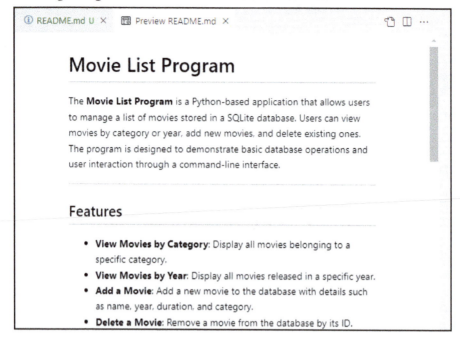

Perspective

This chapter shows that you can use Copilot in other phases of software development, not just the implementation and testing phases. Although the Movie List program is a small sample program, it illustrates how you can use Copilot with the planning, design, and maintenance phases of software development. Typically, these phases become more important as your software grows bigger and more complex.

Terms

markdown
requirements document
README file

Exercises

1. Open the ch06/movie_list_start folder and add documentation for the program. This should include comments for each function as well as a README.md file for the program.

2. Open the ch06/movie_list_start folder and refactor the code to improve it. For example, you may want to reorganize some of the functions into classes. Be sure to update any documentation to reflect the changes.

3. Design a library program that allows users to check out and return books. To start, make decisions about the architecture for this program, including the programming language, the database, and the classes. Then, create a directory structure for this program.

Chapter 7

Implement unit testing

Chapter 3 shows how to use Python's built-in doctest framework to generate simple tests for your functions. Typically, though, it's considered a best practice to use more robust unit testing frameworks like the ones described in this chapter. These frameworks let you store your tests in separate files. This makes it possible to create more thorough tests without making your code files so large that they become difficult to maintain.

This chapter shows how to use Copilot to implement unit tests for two popular frameworks. The first framework implements unit tests for Python code, and the second implements tests for JavaScript. However, the Copilot skills presented in this chapter are similar for most unit testing frameworks. As a result, you only need to read about one of these frameworks, not both, to get an understanding of how to use Copilot to implement unit tests. Then, this chapter shows how to use unit tests to mock external dependencies, and it shows how to implement test-driven development (TDD).

An introduction to unit testing..170

How to unit test Python code 170
Install pytest..171
Generate some initial tests...172
Generate tests for edge cases and more 176
Troubleshoot failing tests...177

How to unit test JavaScript...181
Install Node.js 181
Install Jest...182
Generate some initial tests...184
Generate tests for edge cases and more 188
Troubleshoot failing tests...189

How to mock external dependencies..192
Mock a dependency in Python..193
Mock a dependency in JavaScript 195

How to use test-driven development (TDD) 198
Generate tests for non-existent code..199
Generate code that passes the tests..201
Refactor the code by generating more tests..202

Perspective..205

An introduction to unit testing

Unit testing tests the individual units of a program. Typically, this means testing functions or methods to make sure they behave as expected. In addition, unit testing is typically automated, so the tests are easy to run repeatedly. That way, you can run the tests after a code change to make sure everything still works as expected.

Some benefits of unit testing

- **Improved code quality.** That's because unit tests encourage developers to create modular code that performs data validation and handles edge cases and errors.
- **Early bug detection.** That's because unit tests make it easier to find bugs early before they can affect other parts of the codebase.
- **Easier modification and refactoring.** That's because unit tests provide a way to quickly make sure your changes don't break existing functionality or introduce bugs.
- **Easier debugging.** That's because a failing test gives you info on what and where the bug is.
- **Enhanced documentation.** That's because the descriptive names for the tests document the expected behavior of the code.

If you find that it's hard to test a function, that's often because the function is poorly coded. For instance, it's generally considered a bad practice to code a function that performs more than one task. Such a function is also difficult to test.

To make a function that performs multiple tasks easier to test, you can split it into smaller functions that perform just one task. Then, you can write tests for these smaller functions and rewrite the original function so it's composed of the smaller, tested functions. This improves the function and makes your code more modular and reusable.

How to unit test Python code

Two popular testing frameworks for Python are unittest and pytest.

Two unit testing frameworks for Python

- unittest
- pytest

The unittest framework is a built-in part of the Python language. As a result, you don't need to install it to use it.

By contrast, the pytest framework is a third-party framework. As a result, you need to install it before you can use it. However, VS Code can handle this for you. So, if you're using VS Code, it's easy to install pytest.

Given that both testing frameworks are easy to use in VS Code, which should you choose? Most developers choose pytest because its syntax is simpler, and it offers more features. However, unittest is inspired by JUnit. As a result, it may be a good choice for developers who are familiar with similar unit testing frameworks in other languages. This chapter shows how to use pytest, but most of the skills presented for working with pytest also work with unittest.

Install pytest

To install pytest in VS Code, you must install the Python extension as described in chapter 1. Then, you can open a Python file in the code editor and click the Testing (beaker) icon on the left side of the Explorer window. This should display a Testing window like the one shown next.

VS Code's Testing window before Python tests are configured

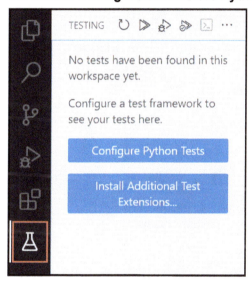

From this Testing window, click the Configure Python Tests button to display the following dialog. You can also display this dialog by selecting View ▶ Command Palette ▶ Python: Configure Tests.

The dialog to choose the Python test framework

From this dialog, select the testing framework you want to use. This should display the following dialog.

The dialog to select the directory for the tests

Use this dialog to select the directory to contain the tests. Typically, you can accept the default choice of the root directory for this dialog.

The Testing window for the Calculator program after pytest is installed

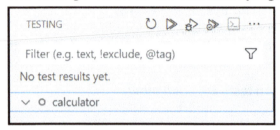

The Testing window has a menu across the top with buttons to work with tests. Two of the most important buttons are shown next.

Two important buttons in the Testing window

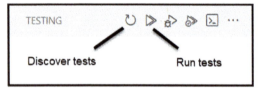

To refresh the tests that display in the Testing window, you can click the Discover button. Then, you can click the Run button to run the tests.

Generate some initial tests

Once you install pytest, you can use Copilot to generate tests for existing Python code. To keep things simple, this chapter uses a basic Calculator program as its main example. This program provides functions to add, subtract, multiply, and divide two numeric values. To start, these functions don't do any data validation or exception handling, and they're stored in a file named calculate.py in a folder named calculator as shown next.

The calculator/calculate.py file

```python
def add(a, b):
    return a + b

def subtract(a, b):
    return a - b

def multiply(a, b):
    return a * b

def divide(a, b):
    return a / b
```

To test this code, I needed to add a file to store the tests, and I needed to generate some tests for that file. To do that, I entered the following prompt in Edit mode.

A prompt to add a file for the Python tests

Add a file for pytests of the functions in calculate.py.

In this prompt, I used "pytests" to specify that the tests should use the pytest framework. If I didn't specify that, Copilot might generate tests that use the unittest framework, even though I configured the project to use pytest.

In response to this prompt, Copilot generated a file named test_calculate.py. This follows the naming convention that pytest expects, where the file that contains tests starts or ends with "test". If you follow this convention, pytest can discover the tests.

Copilot also generated initial tests for the functions in calculate.py as shown next.

The Python tests generated by Copilot

```python
import pytest
from calculate import add, subtract, multiply, divide

def test_add():
    assert add(2, 3) == 5
    assert add(-1, 1) == 0
    assert add(0, 0) == 0

def test_subtract():
    assert subtract(5, 3) == 2
    assert subtract(0, 5) == -5
    assert subtract(-3, -2) == -1

def test_multiply():
    assert multiply(2, 3) == 6
    assert multiply(1.234567, 2) == 2.469134
    assert multiply(0, 5) == 0

def test_divide():
    assert divide(6, 3) == 2
    assert divide(1, 3) == 0.333333
    with pytest.raises(ZeroDivisionError):
        divide(1, 0)
```

In this code, the test named test_divide() expects the divide() function to raise a ZeroDivisionError when a value of zero is passed as a divisor. In other words, if the function throws a ZeroDivisionError, the test passes.

To run the tests, I clicked on the Testing (beaker) icon to open the Testing window. This automatically discovered the tests and displayed their names as shown next. The small round dots indicate the tests haven't been run yet.

The Testing window before running the tests for the first time

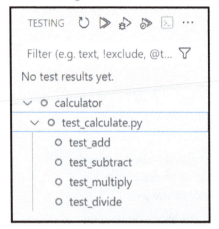

If you don't see any tests, you can click the Discover button. To run the tests shown previously, you can click the Run button.

After a test run completes, the Testing window marks the tests that pass with a green check, and it marks any test that fails with a red X. For example, when I ran the tests, the Testing window marked the tests as shown next.

The Testing window after running the tests

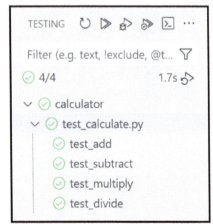

This window shows that all of the tests passed. However, in general, it's a good practice for the name of a test to provide a description of that test, and the names that Copilot generated aren't as descriptive as I would like. To fix this, I entered the following prompt.

A prompt to provide descriptive names for the tests

> Please group the tests by function and rename them to make them more descriptive so they appear clearly in the Testing window.

When I entered this prompt, Copilot split the tests into multiple functions with more descriptive names. For example, it split the tests for the add() function into the following three functions.

The new tests generated by Copilot

```python
def test_add_positive_numbers():
    assert add(2, 3) == 5

def test_add_positive_and_negative():
    assert add(-1, 1) == 0

def test_add_zeros():
    assert add(0, 0) == 0
```

Copilot generated similar functions to test the subtract(), multiply(), and divide() functions. When I ran the new tests, they all passed as shown next.

The Testing window after the new tests run and pass

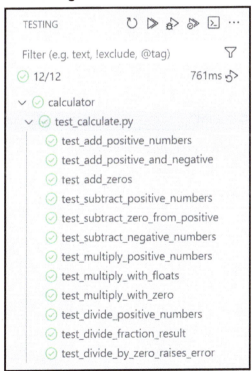

Generate tests for edge cases and more

Once you have your initial tests working, you can ask Copilot to create more tests to cover more cases. To do that, I entered the following prompt in Edit mode.

A prompt that asks for additional tests

> Add more tests for the add() function. Test edge cases, missing arguments, invalid arguments, integers and decimals, data validation, and exception handling.

This prompt generated the following new tests for the add() function.

Some of the additional tests generated by Copilot

```python
def test_add_large_numbers():
    assert add(1_000_000, 2_000_000) == 3_000_000

def test_add_with_decimals():
    assert add(1.5, 2.3) == 3.8

def test_add_negative_and_decimal():
    assert add(-1.5, 2.5) == 1.0

def test_add_missing_arguments():
    with pytest.raises(TypeError):
        add(1)
```

After reviewing these tests, I asked Copilot if it could think of anything else.

A follow-up prompt

> Are there other tests you recommend for the add() function?

In response, Copilot generated tests for floating-point precision issues, adding very small numbers, and mixed data types.

Some of the tests generated by the follow-up prompt

```python
def test_add_floating_point_precision():
    assert add(0.1, 0.2) == pytest.approx(0.3, rel=1e-9)

def test_add_very_small_numbers():
    assert add(1e-10, 1e-10) == 2e-10

def test_add_large_and_small_number():
    assert add(1_000_000, 1e-10) == pytest.approx(1_000_000, rel=1e-9)

def test_add_mixed_integer_and_float():
    assert add(5, 2.5) == 7.5

def test_add_mixed_negative_integer_and_float():
    assert add(-5, 2.5) == -2.5

def test_add_with_complex_numbers():
    with pytest.raises(TypeError):
        add(1 + 2j, 3 + 4j)
```

I accepted the new tests, ran them, and found that some of them failed.

Normally, I'd use Copilot to troubleshoot the failing tests before I generated any more tests, but since this chapter hasn't shown how to troubleshoot failing tests yet, I decided to generate the rest of the tests for the Calculator program first. To do that, I entered the following prompt.

A prompt to generate tests for the rest of the functions

Using the tests for the add() function as a guide, generate tests for the rest of the functions in calculate.py.

When I accepted and ran these new tests, some of them also failed. At this point, I was ready to use Copilot to troubleshoot the failing tests.

Troubleshoot failing tests

When a test fails, it's marked in the Testing window with a red X. For example, the following Testing window shows some of the failing tests for the add() function.

Two failing tests in the Testing window

⊘ test_add_with_boolean
⊗ test_add_with_lists
⊗ test_add_with_tuples
⊘ test_add_with_dictionaries

If you click the red X next to the test name, VS Code displays the code for that test in the code editor, and it marks that code by displaying a red X before the line number. In addition, it marks that code with a red arrow and displays info about the test failure below the function signature.

A failing test in the code editor

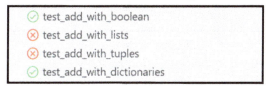

In this example, the test expects the function to throw an error, but the function doesn't do that. I clicked on the red X for all the failing tests, and all but one expect the function to raise a TypeError when the calling code submits invalid data. To fix that, I entered the following prompt in Edit mode.

A prompt to fix the failing tests

Fix the functions in calculate.py so they raise the TypeError expected by the tests.

The updated functions

```python
def add(a, b):
    if not isinstance(a, (int, float)) or not isinstance(b, (int, float)):
        raise TypeError("Both arguments must be int or float")
    return a + b

def subtract(a, b):
    if not isinstance(a, (int, float)) or not isinstance(b, (int, float)):
        raise TypeError("Both arguments must be int or float")
    return a - b

def multiply(a, b):
    if not isinstance(a, (int, float)) or not isinstance(b, (int, float)):
        raise TypeError("Both arguments must be int or float")
    return a * b

def divide(a, b):
    if not isinstance(a, (int, float)) or not isinstance(b, (int, float)):
        raise TypeError("Both arguments must be int or float")
    if b == 0:
        raise ZeroDivisionError("Division by zero is not allowed")
    return a / b
```

I ran the tests again, and all but one of them passed. So, I clicked on the red X next to the one remaining failing test to display it in the code editor as shown next.

One remaining failing test in the code editor

```
⊗ 142      def test_divide_fraction_result():    ⊗ c:\murach\ai\ch7\pytest\calculato

  c:\murach\ai\ch7\pytest\calculator\test_calculate....   test_divid...  ↑ ↓ ⟳ | ≡⤬ ⧉ ×

      c:\murach\ai\ch7\pytest\calculator\test_calculate.py::test_divide
  >           assert divide(1, 3) == 0.333333
  E           assert 0.3333333333333333 == 0.333333
  E           +  where 0.3333333333333333 = divide(1, 3)

  test_calculate.py:143: AssertionError
```

Here, the info displayed in the code editor seems to indicate that the test is encountering some sort of precision error. To fix this issue, I considered using the Chat window to ask Copilot to fix it. However, I decided that it would be easier to get Copilot's input by clicking on the sparkle icon that appears in a pytest when you click the red arrow. This runs the /fix command as shown next.

The sparkle icon for a failing test

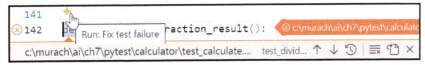

After I clicked on the sparkle icon, Copilot opened the inline chat interface and ran the following /fix command.

The result of the /fix command

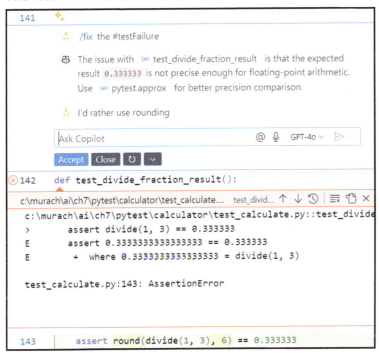

Initially, Copilot suggested updating the test to use the pytest.approx() method. Since I've had some trouble with that in the past, I entered another prompt to tell Copilot that I'd rather use rounding. When I did that, Copilot regenerated its suggested code and displayed it in green below the block with the test failure info.

To accept this suggested code, I clicked the Accept button. Then, I saved the file and ran the tests again. This time, they all passed.

While reviewing this fix, I wondered if it would be better to apply the rounding in the function instead of the test. To get ideas about this, I entered the following prompt in the Chat window in Ask mode.

A prompt that requests a recommendation

> The last edit applied rounding to a test of the divide() function so the test would pass. Would it be better to apply the rounding in the divide() function itself?

When I sent this prompt to Copilot, its response included a detailed explanation of both approaches. To start, the response began by explaining why you might you might want to apply rounding in the function.

The start of the response

 GitHub Copilot

> Used 2 references

It depends on the intended behavior of the  divide() function. Here are the considerations:

Applying Rounding in the  divide() Function

If the  divide() function is meant to always return results rounded to a specific precision (e.g., for financial calculations or other use cases where precision is critical), then applying rounding in the function itself makes sense. For example:

This was followed by suggested code for applying rounding in the function. The response ended by explaining why you might want to keep rounding in the test and by making some recommendations.

The end of the response

Keeping Rounding in the Test

If the  divide() function is intended to return the raw result of the division without any modifications, then rounding should remain in the test. This approach is more flexible, as it allows the function to be used in scenarios where exact precision is required, and the caller can decide how to handle rounding.

This approach ensures the function remains general-purpose and avoids introducing assumptions about precision into the function itself.

Recommendation

- **If rounding is a core requirement of the function's behavior**, apply it in the  divide() function.
- **If the function should remain general-purpose**, keep rounding in the test.

In most cases, keeping the function general-purpose is preferable unless there is a specific requirement for rounding.

After reading this info, I decided that I wanted the function to remain general-purpose. As a result, I didn't need to make any further changes to the code.

How to unit test JavaScript

To implement unit testing in JavaScript, you can use a popular JavaScript testing framework known as Jest. Since Jest uses Node.js to run its tests, you must have Node.js installed to be able to use Jest. Luckily, you can use Copilot and the @terminal chat participant to help you with this.

Install Node.js

You can use the @terminal chat participant to check whether Node.js is already installed on your system. For instance, I entered the following prompt in Ask mode.

A prompt to check if Node.js is installed

@terminal check if node.js is installed

In response, Copilot generated a Terminal command to check for Node.js as shown next.

A response with a command to check for Node.js

To run this command, I hovered the mouse over it and clicked the Insert into Terminal icon. This inserted the command in the Terminal window as shown next. Then I pressed Enter to run the command.

The command in the Terminal window

If this command displays a version number, Node.js is already installed. If it doesn't, you can install Node.js by downloading its installer file from www.nodejs.org and running that file. Then you can run this command again to make sure Node.js installed correctly.

Install Jest

To install Jest for a project, you begin by opening the folder for the project. If VS Code's Explorer window doesn't have a package.json in this folder, you need to add one. You can use the @terminal chat participant for this, too. For instance, I entered the following prompt in Ask mode.

A prompt to add a package.json file

@terminal add a package.json file

In response, Copilot generated an npm command to add a package.json file as shown next.

A response with an npm command to add a package.json file

When you insert this command into the Terminal window and run it, the Explorer window should display a package.json file.

Once you have a package.json file, you can run an npm command to install Jest for the folder. This command updates the package.json file. Once again, you can use the @terminal chat participant to help you. For instance, I entered the following prompt in Ask mode.

A prompt to install Jest

@terminal install jest

In response, Copilot generated the following npm command for installing Jest.

A response with an npm command to install Jest

I inserted this command into the Terminal window and pressed Enter to run the command. When I did, the command installed Jest for the calculator folder that was open in VS Code. This updated the package.json file, and it created the package-lock.json file and the node_modules subfolder.

When you install Jest, the Terminal window may display some deprecation warnings for other packages in your project. These warnings are common, and you can ignore them unless the issues they describe cause problems in your project. In that case, you can ask Copilot to help you troubleshoot.

To install the Jest extension, you can open VS Code's Extensions window and type "jest" in the search box at the top of the window. Then, the Extensions window should display several options. Choose the Jest extension by Orta and click Install as shown next.

The Jest extension

Once you install Jest and the Jest extension, VS Code should display a Testing (beaker) icon that you can click to open the Testing window. However, sometimes VS Code doesn't display the Testing (beaker) icon. If that happens, you can restart VS Code. Or, you can reload the VS Code window.

One way to reload the VS Code window is to use the @vscode chat participant in Copilot. For example, I entered the following prompt in Ask mode.

A prompt to reload a VS Code window

@vscode reload window

When I did that, Copilot displayed the following response.

The response with the Show in Command Palette button

At this point, I clicked the Show in Command Palette button to display the following commands.

The Command Palette with the Developer: Reload Window command

Then, I clicked the Developer: Reload Windows command. When I did that, VS Code reloaded the current window and displayed the Testing (beaker) icon.

When the Testing icon is displayed, you can click it to display the Testing window. For example, I clicked this icon to display the following Testing window.

The Testing window for the Calculator program after Jest is installed

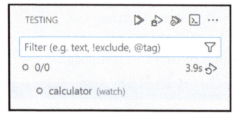

By default, the Jest extension sets Jest in watch mode, as indicated by the (watch) designation after the program name. In watch mode, Jest automatically discovers and runs the tests whenever you save a code file in your project.

Generate some initial tests

Once you install Jest, you can use Copilot to generate tests for existing JavaScript code. To keep things simple, this chapter uses a basic Calculator program as its main example. This program provides functions to add, subtract, multiply, and divide two numeric values. To start, these functions don't do any data validation or exception handling, and they're stored in a file named calculate.js in a folder named calculator as shown next.

The calculator/calculate.js file

```
function add(a, b) {
    return a + b;
}

function subtract(a, b) {
    return a - b;
}

function multiply(a, b) {
    return a * b;
}

function divide(a, b) {
    return a / b;
}
```

The Jest framework uses Node.js to run the tests, and it expects the functions you want to test to be exported in a CommonJS module. So, to test these functions with Jest, I need to add that export.

However, browsers typically can't use CommonJS modules. So, they might throw errors if they encounter a CommonJS export. This shouldn't affect the functioning of your website, but it's good to limit errors if you can. One way to do that is to use a conditional statement with the export. To do that, I entered the following prompt in Edit mode.

A prompt to add a CommonJS export to the calculate.js file

Update calculate.js so it exports all the functions in a CommonJS module.
Use a conditional statement so export only happens if module exists.
Add a comment that the export is for Jest testing.

The code generated by Copilot

```
// Export for Jest testing
if (typeof module !== 'undefined' && module.exports) {
    module.exports = {
        add,
        subtract,
        multiply,
        divide
    };
}
```

Since this code provided the export I needed, I accepted it.

After adding this export to the calculate.js file, I needed to add another file to store the tests, and I needed to generate some starting tests. To do that, I entered the following prompt in Edit mode.

A prompt to add a file for the tests

Add a file for Jest tests of the functions in calculate.js.

The response from Copilot generated a file named calculate.test.js. This follows the naming convention that Jest expects, which is the name of the file being tested, followed by ".test", followed by the file extension. If you follow this convention, Jest can discover the tests. In addition, Copilot generated the following tests.

Unit tests generated by Copilot

```javascript
const { add, subtract, multiply, divide } = require('./calculate');

test('adds two numbers', () => {
    expect(add(2, 3)).toBe(5);
    expect(add(-1, 1)).toBe(0);
});

test('subtracts two numbers', () => {
    expect(subtract(5, 3)).toBe(2);
    expect(subtract(0, 5)).toBe(-5);
});

test('multiplies two numbers', () => {
    expect(multiply(4, 3)).toBe(12);
    expect(multiply(-2, 3)).toBe(-6);
});

test('divides two numbers', () => {
    expect(divide(6, 3)).toBe(2);
    expect(divide(5, 2)).toBeCloseTo(2.5);
});
```

To run the tests, I clicked the Testing (beaker) icon to open the Testing window. Since Jest is in watch mode, it had automatically discovered and ran the tests when I saved the file that contained them. So, the Testing window displayed the results of that test run as shown next.

The Testing window after running the tests for the first time

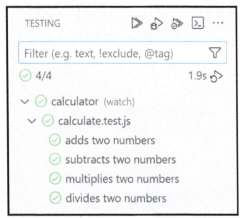

The Testing window marks tests that pass with a green check and tests that don't pass with a red X. In this window, the initial tests passed, which is good.

In addition, this Testing window shows that Copilot generated descriptive names for the tests, which is also good. However, Jest includes a feature that allows it to group similar tests, and I wanted to use that feature to further organize the tests. To do that, I entered the following prompt in Edit mode.

A prompt to group the tests

Please group the tests by function.

Some of the grouping code generated by Copilot

```
// Tests for add function
describe('add', () => {
    test('adds two numbers', () => {
        expect(add(2, 3)).toBe(5);
        expect(add(-1, 1)).toBe(0);
    });
});

// Tests for subtract function
describe('subtract', () => {
    test('subtracts two numbers', () => {
        expect(subtract(5, 3)).toBe(2);
        expect(subtract(0, 5)).toBe(-5);
    });
});
```

When I accepted this code and saved the file, the Testing window displayed the new groups as shown next.

The Testing window with the new groups

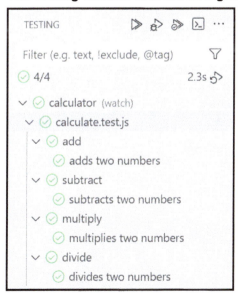

These groups organize the tests by clearly identifying each function that's being tested.

Generate tests for edge cases and more

Once you have your initial tests working, you can ask Copilot to create more tests to cover more options. To do that, I entered the following prompt in Edit mode to expand the tests for the add() function.

A prompt that asks for additional tests

> Add more tests for the add() function. Test edge cases, missing arguments, invalid arguments, integers and decimals, data validation, and exception handling.

In response, Copilot generated many more tests including the ones shown next.

Some of the additional tests generated by Copilot

```
test('handles missing arguments', () => {
    expect(() => add(2)).toThrow();
    expect(() => add()).toThrow();
});

test('handles invalid arguments', () => {
    expect(() => add(2, 'a')).toThrow();
    expect(() => add(null, 3)).toThrow();
    expect(() => add(undefined, undefined)).toThrow();
});

test('adds integers and decimals', () => {
    expect(add(2, 3.5)).toBe(5.5);
    expect(add(-1.2, 1.2)).toBeCloseTo(0);
});
```

Then, I entered another prompt to ask Copilot if it could think of anything else.

A follow-up prompt

> Are there other tests you recommend for the add() function?

In response, Copilot generated tests for adding zero, handling negative numbers, working with very large and very small numbers, and using scientific notation. I noticed that it didn't test for floating-point precision issues, so I entered another prompt to request that. After accepting Copilot's suggestions, I had many more tests including the ones shown next.

Some of the tests generated by the follow-up prompt

```
test('adds very large numbers', () => {
    expect(add(1e15, 1e15)).toBe(2e15);
    expect(add(-1e15, 1e15)).toBe(0);
});

test('adds very small numbers', () => {
    expect(add(1e-15, 1e-15)).toBeCloseTo(2e-15);
    expect(add(-1e-15, 1e-15)).toBeCloseTo(0);
});

test('adds numbers in scientific notation', () => {
```

```
    expect(add(1e3, 2e3)).toBe(3e3);
    expect(add(-1e3, 1e3)).toBe(0);
});

test('handles floating-point precision issues', () => {
    expect(add(0.1, 0.2)).toBeCloseTo(0.3);
    expect(add(0.123456789, 0.987654321)).toBeCloseTo(1.11111111);
});
```

I accepted the new tests, saved the file, and found that some of the new tests failed.

Normally, I'd use Copilot to troubleshoot the failing tests before I generated any more tests, but since this chapter hasn't shown how to troubleshoot failing Jest tests yet, I decided to generate the rest of the tests for the Calculator program first. To do that, I entered the following prompt.

A prompt to generate tests for the rest of the functions

Using the tests for the add() function as a guide, generate tests for the rest of the functions in calculate.js.

When I accepted these new tests and saved the file, some of them also failed. At this point, I was ready to use Copilot to troubleshoot the failing tests.

Troubleshoot failing tests

When a test fails, it's marked in the Testing window with a red X. For example, the following Testing window shows some of the failing tests for the add() function.

Two failing tests in the Testing window

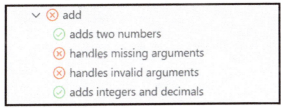

If you click the red X next to the test name, VS Code displays the code for that test in the code editor. It marks that code with a red X before the line number and a red squiggle under the code as shown next.

A failing test in the code editor

```
⊗  10        test('handles missing arguments', () => {
   11            expect(() => add(2)).toThrow();
   12            expect(() => add()).toThrow();
   13        });
```

A Jest test doesn't automatically display info about the test failure. However, you can display this info by placing your mouse over the red squiggle as shown next.

Failure info when the mouse hovers over the red squiggle

```
 2
 3    add > handles missing arguments
 4    -----
 5    Error: expect(received).toThrow()
 6
 7    Received function did not throw Jest
 8
 9    function(): any
10    View Problem...   Quick Fix... ...   Fix using Copil...  () => {
11            expect(() => add(2)).toThrow();
12            expect(() => add()).toThrow();
13        });
```

In this case, the test expects the function to throw an error, but it doesn't. I hovered the mouse over the red squiggle for all the failing tests and found that they all fail for this reason. To fix that, I entered the following prompt in Edit mode.

A prompt to fix the failing tests

> Fix the functions in calculate.js so all the tests pass.

In response, Copilot fixed the functions in the calculate.js file by adding validation that throws the errors expected by the tests as shown next.

The updated functions

```
function add(a, b) {
    if (typeof a !== 'number' || typeof b !== 'number' || isNaN(a) || isNaN(b)) {
        throw new Error('Invalid arguments: both arguments must be numbers');
    }
    return a + b;
}

function subtract(a, b) {
    if (typeof a !== 'number' || typeof b !== 'number' || isNaN(a) || isNaN(b)) {
        throw new Error('Invalid arguments: both arguments must be numbers');
    }
    return a - b;
}

function multiply(a, b) {
    if (typeof a !== 'number' || typeof b !== 'number' || isNaN(a) || isNaN(b)) {
        throw new Error('Invalid arguments: both arguments must be numbers');
    }
    return a * b;
}

function divide(a, b) {
    if (typeof a !== 'number' || typeof b !== 'number' || isNaN(a) || isNaN(b)) {
        throw new Error('Invalid arguments: both arguments must be numbers');
    }
    if (b === 0) {
        throw new Error('Division by zero is not allowed');
    }
    return a / b;
}
```

When I saved the file, most of the tests passed. However, four tests still failed. To figure out why, I clicked the red X next to one of the failing tests and hovered over the red squiggle. When I did, it displayed the following info.

The failing test and the "Fix using Copilot" option

```
 31    add > throws exceptions for invalid inputs
 32
 33    -----                                        ow();
 34    Error: expect(received).toThrow()
 35
 36    Received function did not throw Jest         ts', () => {
 37    View Problem (Al...   Quick Fix... (C...   Fix using Copilot (...
 38          expect(() => add(Infinity, -Infinity)).toThrow();
 39       });
```

Unfortunately, this info didn't tell me anything new. So, to get more info, I clicked the "Fix using Copilot" option at the bottom right of the dialog. This ran the following /fix command.

The result of the /fix command

```
 36    test('throws exceptions for invalid inputs', () => {
 37        expect(() => add(NaN, 2)).toThrow();
```

/fix add > throws exceptions for invalid inputs

Error: expect(received).toThrow()

Received function did not throw

The issue is that the [•] add function does not throw an exception when adding [•] Infinity and -Infinity. To fix this, you need to update the [•] add function in the ʲˢ calculate.js file to handle this case and throw an error.

```
function add(a, b) {
    if (typeof a !== 'number' || type(      ber') {
        throw new Error('Invalid arguments ); Apply in Editor
    }
    if (!isFinite(a) || !isFinite(b)) {
        throw new Error('Invalid arguments: cannot add Inf
    }
    return a + b;
}
```

Ask Copilot   @ 🎤 GPT-4o ∨ ▷

[Close] [View in Chat] [↻] [∨]

```
 38        expect(() => add(Infinity, -Infinity)).toThrow();
 39     });
```

To apply this change to the add() function, I could have clicked the Apply in Editor icon. Instead, I checked whether the three other tests fail because they subtract, multiply, and divide Infinity and –Infinity, and they do.

In other words, all four calculator functions need to be updated. So, I thought it would be more efficient to use the Chat window to fix them all at once. To do that, I entered the following prompt in Edit mode.

A prompt to fix the failing tests for infinite values

> Update the functions to check that each argument is finite.

In response, Copilot generated code that threw the error expected by the test if any infinite arguments are passed to the tests. When I accepted and saved the changes, Jest automatically ran the tests, and they all passed!

How to mock external dependencies

Chapter 3 showed how to simulate user input and random numbers in Python doctests. This is called *mocking*, and it's commonly used in unit testing for things that are nondeterministic, like random numbers. That way, you can be sure your tests return consistent, repeatable results every time they run.

When writing unit tests, it's also common to mock external dependencies. An *external dependency* is anything that your code depends on that isn't part of the code for your project. Examples of external dependencies include accessing a file, a database, or a web API. This section shows how to use Copilot to mock accessing a file in both Python and JavaScript.

Mocking external dependencies provides the following benefits.

Some benefits of mocking external dependencies

- **Code isolation.** You can focus on testing the code in the function since you don't need to test the code that accesses an external dependency such as a file, database, or web API.
- **Test reliability.** Your tests still work correctly even if the external dependency isn't working correctly.
- **Faster test runs.** Code that mocks external dependencies typically runs faster than code that actually uses external dependencies.
- **Improved edge cases.** It's easy to mock situations that rarely occur and would be hard to test in real life such as an operating system error.
- **Easier maintainance.** It's easier to set up, update, and tear down tests.

To illustrate how this works, this chapter presents an example that gets an exchange rate from the following text file.

The exchange_rates.json file

```json
{
    "EUR": 1.1,
    "JPY": 0.007,
    "GBP": 1.25,
    "AUD": 0.66,
    "CAD": 0.75,
    "CNY": 0.14
}
```

To start, this chapter shows how to mock a dependency on this file in a Python function. Then, it shows how to do the same thing with in a JavaScript function.

Mock a dependency in Python

The following Python function depends on the exchange_rates.json file. In other words, the JSON file is an external dependency for the function.

The convert_to_usd() function

```python
import json
def convert_to_usd(amount, currency):
    with open("exchange_rates.json") as f:
        rates = json.load(f)
    if currency not in rates:
        return None
    rate = rates[currency]
    return amount * rate
```

To generate a test for this function, I entered the following prompt in Edit mode.

A prompt to test the convert_to_usd() function with mocking

Task: Add tests for convert_to_usd(). Mock the calls to open().

Specs:
Test when the file opens successfully.
Test when the file fails to open.
Test when the file isn't found.

In response, Copilot generated the following tests.

The pytests generated by Copilot

```python
from unittest.mock import patch

def test_convert_to_usd_file_opens_successfully():
    with patch("builtins.open", create=True) as mock_open:
        mock_open.return_value.__enter__.return_value.read.return_value = (
            '{"EUR": 1.1, "GBP": 1.25}'
        )
        assert round(convert_to_usd(100, "EUR"), 2) == 110.00
```

```
def test_convert_to_usd_file_unable_to_open():
    with patch("builtins.open", side_effect=OSError("Unable to open file")):
        with pytest.raises(OSError, match="Unable to open file"):
            convert_to_usd(100, "EUR")

def test_convert_to_usd_file_not_found():
    with patch("builtins.open", side_effect=FileNotFoundError("File not found")):
        with pytest.raises(FileNotFoundError, match="File not found"):
            convert_to_usd(100, "EUR")
```

From the function names, I could tell that these tests mock opening the file successfully, not being able to open the file, and not being able to find the file. However, I was curious about the code that returns a value in the test that mocks opening the file successfully. So, I selected that code, right-clicked it, and selected Copilot ▶ Explain from the context menu. When I did, Copilot's response began by displaying the prompt and the selected code.

The prompt and the selected code

@workspace /explain Write an explanation for the active selection as paragraphs of text.

```
mock_open.return_value.__enter__.return_value.read.return_value = (
        '{"EUR": 1.1, "GBP": 1.25}'
    )
```

Then, the response continued by explaining the selected code as shown next.

The explanation of the selected code

⏣ GitHub Copilot

The provided line of code configures the behavior of the `mock_open` object, which is used to simulate the behavior of the `open` function in Python. Specifically, it sets up the return value for when the file is read within a `with` statement.

- `mock_open.return_value` refers to the object that is returned when the `open` function is called.
- `.__enter__()` is invoked when the `with` statement is entered, as part of the context manager protocol.
- `.__enter__.return_value.read()` simulates the behavior of calling the `read()` method on the file object returned by `open`.
- `.return_value = '{"EUR": 1.1, "GBP": 1.25}'` specifies that when the `read()` method is called, it will return the string `'{"EUR": 1.1, "GBP": 1.25}'`.

This string represents a JSON object containing exchange rates for two currencies: `"EUR"` (Euro) with a rate of `1.1` and `"GBP"` (British Pound) with a rate of `1.25`. By mocking this behavior, the test can simulate reading exchange rate data from a file without actually requiring the file to exist. This allows the test to focus on verifying the functionality of the `convert_to_usd` function in isolation.

After reading this explanation, I had a better understanding of how that code works, and I realized that I could use similar techniques to mock other types of external dependencies.

Mock a dependency in JavaScript

The following JavaScript function depends on the exchange_rates.json file. In other words, the JSON file is an external dependency for the function.

The convertToUSD() function

```
async function convertToUSD(amount, currency) {
    const response = await fetch('exchange_rates.json');
    if (!response.ok) {
        throw new Error('Failed to fetch exchange rates: ' +
            `${response.status} ${response.statusText}`);
    }
    const rates = await response.json();
    const rate = rates[currency];
    if (!rate) {
        throw new Error('Currency not found');
    }
    return amount * rate;
}
```

When JavaScript runs in a browser, it can't directly open a file on the server. That's why this function uses the fetch() method to open the file. This is the same method that JavaScript can use to access a web API on a remote server.

In this example, the exchange_rates.json file is in the same folder as the file that contains the JavaScript. As a result, the code only needs to specify the name of the JSON file, not a path to it.

In addition, when you use fetch() to open a file like this, it won't work if you run the web page from the file system. In that case, JavaScript will return a CORS (Cross-Origin Resource Sharing) error. To fix that, you need to run the web page from a web server. One easy way to do that is to install the following Live Server extension in VS Code.

The Live Server extension

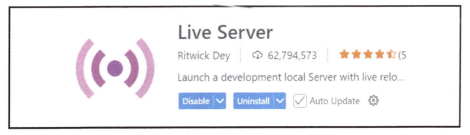

Then, you can right-click the HTML file and select "Open with Live Server" to run the web page from a local development web server as shown next.

The menu for running the web page from a web server

Open with Live Server	Alt+L Alt+O
Stop Live Server	Alt+L Alt+C
Open In Default Browser	Alt+B
Open In Other Browsers	Shift+Alt+B
Command Palette...	Ctrl+Shift+P

If this menu doesn't include "Open with Live Server", you may need to restart VS Code. In addition, if the web browser can't display the page, you may need to use VS Code to select File ▶ Preferences ▶ Settings ▶ Use Local IP as Host.

To generate tests for the JavaScript function, I entered the following prompt in Edit mode.

A prompt to test the convertToUSD() function with mocking

Task: Add tests for convertToUSD(). Mock the calls to fetch().

Specs:
Test when the file opens successfully.
Test when the file fails to open.
Test when the file isn't found.

In response, Copilot generated the following tests.

The Jest tests generated by Copilot

```javascript
describe('convertToUSD', () => {
    beforeEach(() => {
        global.fetch = jest.fn();
    });

    afterEach(() => {
        jest.resetAllMocks();
    });

    test('converts amount to USD using exchange rate', async () => {
        global.fetch.mockResolvedValueOnce({
            ok: true,
            json: async () => ({ EUR: 1.1, GBP: 1.3 }),
        });

        const result = await convertToUSD(100, 'EUR');
        expect(result).toBeCloseTo(110);
    });

    test('throws error if fetch fails', async () => {
        global.fetch.mockResolvedValueOnce({
            ok: false,
            status: 500,
            statusText: 'Internal Server Error',
```

```
    });

    await expect(convertToUSD(100, 'EUR')).rejects.toThrow(
        'Failed to fetch exchange rates: 500 Internal Server Error');
});

test('throws error if file is not found', async () => {
    global.fetch.mockResolvedValueOnce({
        ok: false,
        status: 404,
        statusText: 'Not Found',
    });

    await expect(convertToUSD(100, 'EUR')).rejects.toThrow(
        'Failed to fetch exchange rates: 404 Not Found');
});
});
```

As I reviewed this code, I became curious about how it works. So, I selected the code that I was most curious about, right-clicked it, and selected Copilot ▶ Explain from the context menu. When I did, the response began by displaying the prompt and the selected code.

The prompt and the selected code

```
@workspace /explain Write an explanation for the active selection as paragraphs of text.

beforeEach(() => {
        global.fetch = jest.fn();
    });
    afterEach(() => {
        jest.resetAllMocks();
    });
    test('converts amount to USD using exchange rate', async () => {
        global.fetch.mockResolvedValueOnce({
            ok: true,
            json: async () => ({ EUR: 1.1, GBP: 1.3 }),
        });
        const result = await convertToUSD(100, 'EUR');
        expect(result).toBeCloseTo(110);
    });
```

Then, the response continued with the following explanation of the selected code.

The explanation of the selected code

> **⊕ GitHub Copilot**
>
> This code snippet is part of a Jest test suite for the `convertToUSD` function. It includes a `beforeEach` block, an `afterEach` block, and a test case.
>
> 1. `beforeEach` **Block**: This block is executed before each test in the suite. It sets up a mock implementation of the global `fetch` function using `jest.fn()`. This ensures that any network requests made during the tests are intercepted and handled by the mock, allowing for controlled testing of the `convertToUSD` function without making actual HTTP requests.
> 2. `afterEach` **Block**: This block is executed after each test in the suite. It resets all mocks using `jest.resetAllMocks()`. This ensures that the mock state does not persist between tests, preventing potential interference or unexpected behavior in subsequent tests.
> 3. **Test Case**: The test case verifies that the `convertToUSD` function correctly converts an amount to USD using a mocked exchange rate. The mock implementation of `fetch` is configured to resolve with a response object containing an `ok` property set to `true` and a `json` method that returns a mock exchange rate object (`{ EUR: 1.1, GBP: 1.3 }`). The test calls `convertToUSD` with an amount of `100` and the currency `'EUR'`. It then asserts that the result is approximately `110` (100 multiplied by the exchange rate of 1.1). This ensures that the function behaves as expected when provided with valid input and a successful response from the mocked `fetch` call.

As these examples show, the code to mock external dependencies can be complex. In addition, the tests Copilot generates for you may not work correctly at first, or they may not test exactly what you want. Fortunately, Copilot can help you fix the tests it generates, and it can help you understand them.

How to use test-driven development (TDD)

Test-driven development (TDD) is a methodology where you write the tests for the code first. Then, you write code that passes the tests and nothing more. Once the code passes the tests, you can refactor it to make it work better while still passing all the tests it, or you can refactor it by adding new tests for additional functionality.

Since TDD is based on unit testing, it provides many of the same benefits as unit testing. In addition, it provides the following benefits.

Some benefits of TDD

- **Enhanced collaboration.** Writing the tests first helps all of the developers of a project to clarify the requirements and focus on writing code that implements the requirements and no more.

- **Improved test coverage.** Writing the tests first makes sure that all code is tested. Writing the tests after the code has been written doesn't always test all of the code.

- **Easier refactoring.** That's because refactoring is part of the methodology.

Generate tests for non-existent code

With TDD, you start by writing the tests. For instance, this chapter presents an example that shows how to generate tests for a file that contains functions that manipulate strings. This example uses pytest, but the same concepts apply to other unit testing frameworks such as Jest.

To start, I created a blank file named string_manip.py to store the functions that manipulate strings. Then, I entered the following prompt in Edit mode to create the test file.

A prompt to create the test file

Add a file for pytests for the functions in string_manip.py.

In response, Copilot created a new file with the proper naming convention as shown next.

A response that creates the test file

⊗ GitHub Copilot

test_string_manip.py

Create a new file to add pytest tests for the functions in `string_manip.py`.

⊕ test_string_manip.py **+17 -1**

In addition, within the test file, Copilot generated the following tests.

The tests generated by Copilot

```python
import pytest
from string_manip import *  # Import functions from string_manip.py

# Example test for a function named 'reverse_string'
def test_reverse_string():
    assert reverse_string("hello") == "olleh"
    assert reverse_string("") == ""
    assert reverse_string("a") == "a"

# Example test for a function named 'capitalize_words'
def test_capitalize_words():
    assert capitalize_words("hello world") == "Hello World"
    assert capitalize_words("python programming") == "Python Programming"
    assert capitalize_words("") == ""

# Add more tests for other functions as needed
```

This code begins by importing all the functions from the string_manip.py file. Then, it creates unit tests for functions named reverse_string() and capitalize_words().

Since the string_manip.py file doesn't yet contain functions, Copilot guessed what tests might be needed based on the name of the file. If Copilot can't guess what functions a file might contain, it sometimes generates a generic example test like the one shown next.

A generic example test

```python
def test_some_function():
    assert some_function("input") == "expected_output"
    assert some_function("another_input") == "another_expected_output"
```

After Copilot generates a test file with example tests, you can delete the tests you don't want. Then, you can use Copilot to modify and add new tests.

For example, of the two tests that Copilot generated for the test_string_manip.py file, I decided I didn't want to keep the test for the reverse_string() function. So, I opened the code editor and deleted the test for that function.

On the other hand, I decided to keep the test for the capitalize_words() function. However, I wanted to make some changes. To do that, I entered the following prompt in Edit mode.

A prompt to modify the capitalize test

Refactor the unit test for capitalize_words() so the first two assert statements are in a test for basic operations and the last assert statement is in a test for empty strings.

When I did that, Copilot suggested some changes, and I accepted them to get the following code.

The code that Copilot generated

```python
def test_capitalize_words_basic_operations():
    assert capitalize_words("hello world") == "Hello World"
    assert capitalize_words("python programming") == "Python Programming"

def test_capitalize_words_empty_string():
    assert capitalize_words("") == ""
```

Then, I ran the tests. Because there aren't any functions in the string_manip.py file yet, they failed as shown next.

The failing tests

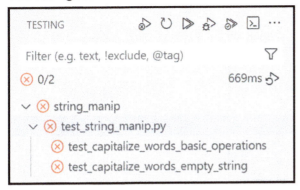

But, at this point, you want the tests to fail because that's how TDD works! First, you write tests that fail. Then, you write code that makes the tests pass. Then, you refactor as needed.

This process is sometimes called *red-green-refactor*. First, the failing tests display in red. Second, the passing tests display in green. Third, you refactor the code as necessary. In the refactor step, you can start the process over by writing a new test that fails.

Generate code that passes the tests

Now that I had two simple tests that were failing, I entered the following prompt in Edit mode to generate code that passes the tests.

A prompt to generate code that passes the tests

Add a capitalize_words() function to string_manip.py that passes the tests in test_string_manip.py.

The function that Copilot generated

```python
def capitalize_words(text):
    """
    Capitalizes the first letter of each word in the given text.
    """
    return " ".join(word.capitalize() for word in text.split())
```

At this point, I accepted and saved the changes and ran the tests again. This time, they passed as shown next.

The tests in the Testing window

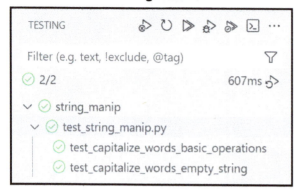

Since the tests provide Copilot with the context it needs, Copilot is often able to generate code that passes the tests without further context.

Refactor the code by generating more tests

Now, this chapter shows how to refactor the capitalize_words() function by adding a test to handle non-string arguments. To do that, I entered the following prompt in Edit mode.

A prompt to test for non-string arguments

Add a test for non-string arguments. Include assert statements for a list, a tuple, an object, an array, and None.

The new test that Copilot generated

```python
def test_capitalize_words_non_string_arguments():
    with pytest.raises(AttributeError):
        capitalize_words(['hello', 'world'])  # List
    with pytest.raises(AttributeError):
        capitalize_words(('hello', 'world'))  # Tuple
    with pytest.raises(AttributeError):
        capitalize_words(object())  # Object
    with pytest.raises(AttributeError):
        capitalize_words(None)  # None
    with pytest.raises(AttributeError):
        capitalize_words(bytearray(b"hello world"))  # Array
```

I accepted and saved the code and ran the tests. As expected, the new test failed.

The new test in the Testing window

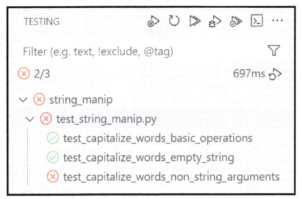

At this point, I entered the following prompt in Edit mode to update the function to make it pass the new test.

A prompt to make the function pass the new test

Update the capitalize_word() function so all the tests pass.

The updated function

```python
def capitalize_words(text):
    """
    Capitalizes the first letter of each word in the given text.
    Raises a TypeError if the input is not a string.
    """
    if not isinstance(text, str):
        raise TypeError("Input must be a string")
    return " ".join(word.capitalize() for word in text.split())
```

I accepted and saved the code and ran the tests. Unexpectedly, the new test still failed.

Since the new test has several assert statements, I wasn't sure which one was failing. To determine this, I considered using the debugger to debug the new test. That's because you can debug a test just as you'd debug any other code.

Instead, I decided it would be better to split the test into multiple tests. That's because it's a good practice for each test to test just one thing whenever that's possible. To do that, I entered the following prompt and got the following response.

A prompt to refactor the non-string argument test

Refactor the test_capitalize_words_non_string_arguments test so each assert statement is in a test with a descriptive name.

The refactored tests generated by Copilot

```python
def test_capitalize_words_with_list():
    with pytest.raises(TypeError):
        capitalize_words(['hello', 'world'])

def test_capitalize_words_with_tuple():
    with pytest.raises(TypeError):
        capitalize_words(('hello', 'world'))

def test_capitalize_words_with_object():
    with pytest.raises(TypeError):
        capitalize_words(object())

def test_capitalize_words_with_none():
    with pytest.raises(TypeError):
        capitalize_words(None)

def test_capitalize_words_with_bytearray():
    with pytest.raises(TypeError):
        capitalize_words(bytearray(b"hello world"))
```

When I accepted the code and ran the tests, they all passed as shown next.

The new tests in the Testing window

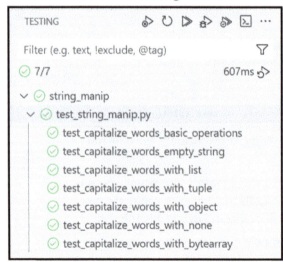

I split the long test into several shorter tests because I thought it would help me determine how to fix the capitalize_word() function. Instead, the shorter tests showed me that the problem was in the test, not in the function being tested. This is one of several reasons why short tests often work better than long ones.

Perspective

This chapter showed how to use Copilot to develop unit tests for your code, including how to mock code that works with external dependencies like files, databases, or APIs. It also showed how to use Copilot with test-driven development, where you generate the unit tests first and then generate the code that passes those tests. Although the testing scenarios presented in this chapter aren't as complex as real-world scenarios, the concepts and skills presented in this chapter provide a good foundation for using Copilot to implement unit testing.

Terms

unit testing

mocking

external dependencies

test-driven development (TDD)

red-green-refactor

Exercises

1. Write pytests for the calculate_future_value() function in the ch01/python folder.
2. Write Jest tests for the getFutureValue() function in the ch07/jest/future_value folder. Note that this function calls another function to perform the calculation.
3. Write Jest tests for the fetchUsers() function in the ch07/jest/users folder. Note that this function calls a web API named JSONPlaceholder. Mock the code that calls the API.
4. Use test-driven development to add more string manipulation functions to the string_manip.py file in the ch07/pytest/string_manip folder.

Index

/clear command, 52
/doc command, 163
/explain command, 52-53
/fix command, 52-53, 179, 191-192
/help command, 52
/new command, 52
@workspace chat participant, 48-49
@vscode chat participant, 48-49
@terminal chat participant, 48, 50, 181-182
@github chat participant, 48, 50

A

Agent mode (Chat), 42
AI
    agent, 5
    assistant, 5
    model components, 6-7
applying suggested code to files, 77-78
architecture, 151
    get feedback, 153
    project structure, 154-155
artificial intelligence (AI), 4
Ask mode (Chat), 38-39

B

benefits of unit testing, 170
bias, 34
book files, 7
Browse Data tab (DB Browser), 129, 142

C

chain of thought prompting, 61-62
chat
    extension, 47
    participant, 47-51
    window, 12
ChatGPT, 5
Claude, 5
commands (Chat), 12
comment prompts, 44-45
configure pytest, 171-172
constraint-based prompting, 56
context, 6, 55

context window, 7, 55
Copilot, 5
    Chat window, 12
    commands, 12
    create Python program, 25-31
    create web app, 12-20
    enable, 8
    extensions, 12
copyright infringement, 33
cutoff date, 34

D

DB Browser for SQLite, 128
deep learning, 4
dependency mocking, 192-198
deterministic, 6
doctest, 68-71

E

edge case, 176
edit files with Copilot, 38-46
Edit mode (Chat), 40-42
explain (Chat), 73
extensions, 12
external dependency, 192-198

F

few-shot prompt, 58-59
find
    bugs, 159-160
    security issues, 160-161
fix
    bugs, 159-160
    image scaling, 111-112
    menu for small screens, 113-117
    responsive design issues, 111-117
    security issues, 160-161
    tests, 177-179
    web content issues, 107
    web header issues, 109-110
    web shared code, 108-109

G

generate
    code, 12
    code for existing tests, 201-202
    database script, 140-141

generate (continued)
    doctest, 70-71
    initial code, 74-76
    SELECT statement, 132-135
    tests (edge cases), 176, 188-189
    tests (Jest), 184-185
    tests (non-existent code), 199-201
    tests (pytest), 172-173
generative AI, 4
generative pretrained transformer (GPT), 4

H

hallucinations, 33

I

inline chat, 43-44
install
    book files, 7
    Jest, 182-184
    Node.js, 181
    pytest, 171
    Python, 9
    VS Code, 8
instructions file (Copilot), 11

J

JavaScript, 181-192
    mock dependency, 195-196
Jest framework, 181-192
    generate tests, 184-185

L

large language model (LLM), 4
Live Server extension, 195-196
LLM problems, 33-34

M

machine learning (ML), 4
markdown language, 163-166
mistakes, 33
mock dependency,
    JavaScript, 195-196
    Python, 193-194
mocking, 192-198
model, 6-7

N

natural language processing (NLP), 4
Node.js, 181-192
nondeterministic, 6

O

one-shot prompt, 58-59

P

planning systems, 7
problems with LLMs, 33-34
prompt, 5
    chaining, 59-61
    engineering, 54-57
pytest framework, 170-180
    generate tests, 172-173
    mock dependency, 193-194
    run tests, 174
    update test names, 175
Python, 9

R

README.md file, 163-166
reasoning systems, 7
red-green-refactor, 201
refactor, 94-97
requirements, 144
requirements document, 147-149
response, 5
retrieval augmented generation (RAG), 62
roles, 56
run doctests, 69-70, 79-81
run pytests, 174

S

schema, 131
self-consistency sampling, 62
set up VS Code, 9-11
simulate random numbers, 71-72
simulate user input, 71-72
slash command (Chat), 47, 51-53
SQLite, 128
structured prompting, 57
summarize code files, 158
summarize data, 138
switch Chat modes, 40

T

test
    code, 20-21, 27-28
    database, 142
    SELECT statement, 133
test-driven development (TDD), 198-204
token, 4
tools, 7
tree-of-thought prompting, 62
troubleshoot tests, 177-179, 189-191

U

unit testing, 68, 170
unittest framework, 170

V

version control, 156
Visual Studio Code, *see VS Code*
VS Code, 8-11

WXYZ

working memory, 6
zero-shot prompt, 58
zero-shot chain of thought prompt, 62

Epilogue

Congratulations on finishing this book! We hope it has helped you to get started with using Copilot to assist you with your programming. If you liked it and want to learn more about programming, Murach also has books on the following subjects.

Web development

HTML/CSS

Modern JavaScript

JavaScript and jQuery

PHP and MySQL

ASP.NET Core MVC

Programming languages

Python

Java

C#

C++

Databases

MySQL

SQL Server

Oracle

Data science

Python for Data Science

R for Data Analysis

For more info, please visit us at www.murach.com.

100% Guarantee

When you order directly from us, you must be satisfied. Try our books for 30 days or our eBooks for 14 days. They must work better than any other programming training you've ever used, or you can return them for a prompt refund. No questions asked!

Mike Murach, Publisher

Ben Murach, President

We want to hear from you

Do you have any comments, questions, or compliments to pass on to us? It would be great to hear from you! Please share your feedback in whatever way works best.

Email: murachbooks@murach.com

Phone: 1-800-221-5528 (Weekdays, 8 am to 4 pm Pacific Time)

Facebook: facebook.com/murachbooks

Instagram: instagram.com/murachbooks

X: x.com/murachbooks

LinkedIn: linkedin.com/company/mike-murach-&-associates

What software you need for this book

- **VS Code.** This book shows how to use Copilot from within Visual Studio Code, an excellent code editor that you can use to develop code in most languages including Python, JavaScript, HTML/CSS, and SQL.
- **Python.** This book shows how to use Copilot to generate Python code. To test this generated code, you need to have Python installed on your system.
- **Any web browser.** This book shows how to use Copilot to generate HTML, CSS, and JavaScript. To test this code, you need to have a web browser.
- **DB Browser for SQLite.** This book shows how to use Copilot to generate standard SQL that works with a database. To test this code, you can use DB Browser for SQLite to run these SQL statements against an embedded SQLite database.

This software can all be downloaded from the internet for free.

What the downloadable files include

- The code presented in this book
- The starting points for the exercises at the end of each chapter

How to download the files for this book

1. Go to www.murach.com.
2. Navigate to the page for *AI-Assisted Programming with Copilot.*
3. Scroll down to the "FREE downloads" tab and click it.
4. Click the Download Now button for the zip file. This should download a zip file.
5. Double-click the zip file to extract the files for this book into a folder named copilot.

For more details, please see chapter 1.